A Servant Leader's Journey

LESSONS FROM LIFE

JIM BOYD

PAULIST PRESS
New York/Mahwah, NJ

Cover design by Sharyn Banks
Book design by Lynn Else

Library of Congress Cataloging-in-Publication Data

Boyd, Jim, 1939-2007.
    A servant leader's journey : lessons from life / Jim Boyd.
        p. cm.
    Includes bibliographical references (p.   ).
    ISBN 978-0-8091-4568-3 (alk. paper)
    1. Boyd, Jim, 1939–2007. 2. Educators—United States—Biography.
3. Amyotrophic lateral sclerosis—Patients—United States—Biography.
I. Title.
    LA2317.B5678A3 2008
    370.92—dc22
    [B]

                                                                    2008028874

Published by Paulist Press
997 Macarthur Boulevard
Mahwah, New Jersey 07430

www.paulistpress.com

Printed and bound in the
United States of America

Contents

Foreword

When I first met Jim Boyd in 2000, he and his wife, Veleda, had just taken early retirement from their jobs in higher education and had started new lives on their Texas Hill Country ranch. To describe it as a ranch, given the neglected state they had found it in when they moved in two years earlier, was a bit of a Texas stretch. It was actually a four-room rock hunting cabin on 725 rugged acres in Mason County. Thirty-five miles from the nearest stoplight and two miles from the nearest neighbor, the ranch had been in Veleda's family for 120 years. It needed a tremendous amount of work.

Jim and Veleda were still in their fifties. She had left her university professorship in the English department of Tarleton State University; he had retired as president of Weatherford College. He told me what he had told his board of regents when he announced his retirement: "I wanted to do something different while I could still put a saddle on a good horse."

He would be busy, that's for sure. In addition to the education consulting he would be doing, he had a historical novel he'd long wanted to write. He would be remodeling the house and building an addition, constructing rock fences by hand, chopping out the ubiquitous Hill Country cedar, planting native grasses, repairing a windmill, clearing out a natural spring, shoring up a stock tank, and getting a good herd of black cattle established on the land. His new life, so different from what he had known for thirty-five years as an educator, would be part of an all-consuming, soul-satisfying effort to bring the ranch back to good, productive life.

He did all that, and more. The novel, *Companions of the Blest*, came out in 2002, but what he had not expected to do was to write a book about his own demise. In the spring of 2004, a mere six years after he and Veleda had moved to the ranch, he was diagnosed with amyotrophic lateral sclerosis. Better known as Lou Gehrig's disease, ALS is a progressive neurological illness that attacks nerve cells responsible for controlling voluntary muscles. Like the legendary Yankee Hall of Famer who lent his name to the illness, Jim, over a period of months, perhaps years, would slowly and inexorably lose all physical function. There is no cure.

The old German settlers knew how to use what was available to them in the sparse Texas Hill Country. So did Jim. He resolved to wring from his illness all that he could to enrich the remainder of his life and the lives of his loved ones. That included writing a second book.

A Servant Leader's Journey is, in Jim's words, "a collection of thoughts from my own imperfect life." Written for his four young grandchildren in the hope that in years to come they would "know something of your Opa other than what you might remember," the book intersperses recollections of his childhood, observations about current events, and reports about the steady progression of the disease. It also offers lessons he learned over the years about leadership, his area of research and expertise as an educator.

Written in diary form, the book is quiet, reserved, thoughtful—just like the author. When he could no longer hide the truth from Veleda, for example, he arranged to tell her, not at home or in other special locales they had enjoyed together in their forty-three years of marriage, but in an anonymous motel room. "I picked this place because I did not want this message to mar the memories of any of the special places in our lives," he wrote. "I cannot write more, because there are no words descriptive of that moment."

A couple of months later, he was working atop a windmill. "It could be said that a person with ALS has no business on a tower thirty feet in the air," he acknowledged. "On the other hand, if you have the strength to get there, what better place for an ALS patient to be than on the top of a windmill? The view from a place you will likely never return to is always the best."

He didn't give up hope, he assured his grandchildren some months after his diagnosis, but it was hope of a different order that sustained him. "My hope now," he wrote, "is that I will have the courage to face this thing with dignity. My hope today is that I will be able to look beyond myself to the beauty in this world."

He wrote about two mind-enhancing experiences he had known during his slightly more than six decades on this earth. The first was the birth of his children; the second was the process of writing his novel. It opened "my eyes to things I have never seen before," he wrote.

And then, he wrote, a third mind-enhancing experience manifested itself, even as the illness began to take control. "To know there is a limited amount of time for you to see anything changes your mind on how you see everything," he wrote. "The dark cloud is still there, but I see everything now with an intensity I never imagined possible. Nothing now is ordinary."

"We had a lot we wanted to get done while we were still able to do so," Jim told me one late summer afternoon a couple of years after moving to the Hill Country. He was sitting in an easy chair in the Boyds' comfortable, book-lined living room. He and Veleda had transformed the old hunting cabin into a comfortable, tastefully decorated ranch house. Behind him, outside the front window, I could see hummingbirds flitting about a feeder on the shady porch. A jackrabbit bobbed along in a leisurely way through the grass just outside the fenced-in yard.

Recalling that moment today, I also recall a saying from the old German settlers who worked the Hill Country land several generations before the Boyds: *Es wird hier mal anders.* "Things will change here someday," the settlers told themselves. And so they have, for Jim and for his friends and family. And so they will for us all.

A Servant Leader's Journey is a gift from a wise man. It is a trustworthy and honest guide from a man who, facing the implacable end of all he cherished, chose to reach out, to share, to love.

Joe Holley
Washington, DC

Preface

I have written this work for a readership of four, my grandchildren: Christian, age five; Mariah, age four; Thomas, age three; and newborn Elisabeth Rose. You are a bit young for it now, but I hope sometime in the future you might see some value in what is written here. I began collecting these thoughts for you shortly after I learned that I had ALS. I knew then that my time with you would be limited, and I wanted you to know something of your Opa other than what you might remember.

There are important lessons that come from every life. What I have written here is a collection of thoughts from my own imperfect life, which has spanned more than a half century. On the pages that follow, there will be stories of joy, hope, despair, success, failure, and enduring love. There are also stories here from the land that has shaped our family culture from frontier times.

In what seems like another lifetime, I spent a great deal of time teaching aspiring leaders and assisting organizations intent on learning more about leadership. Interspersed in this piece are stories about leadership collected from lectures and writings I have done over the years. I give them as a gift to you, not to shape your minds, but to activate your own critical thinking for the decisions you will deal with in your own lives.

There is a presence of the past in all of us. Those who choose to become searchers often find that by looking at the past we can get a much clearer view of the future.

Acknowledgments

This book would likely not have been published were it not for the efforts of Larry Spears, and I am grateful for his help in navigating the sometimes-choppy waters of the publishing world. He is truly a servant leader.

I thank Jack Lowe, Dr. Dennis McCabe, Dr. Mike Moses, Mary Gordon Spence, Patty Taylor, and Dr. Barry Thompson. All provided thoughtful comments on an earlier draft as well as publishing advice, and generally helped more than they had to. I am particularly grateful to Dr. Bill Larmer, whose painstaking review of the manuscript added clarity and strength to the final product. Bob Ferguson, Dr. John Horn, Mike Murray, and Scott Zesch provided materials and counsel that helped bring substance and structure to my efforts.

I thank my family for their help, support, time, and energy throughout this process. I am also indebted to the many individuals who have provided thoughtful comments, timely resources, and encouragement along the way.

Introduction

How do you tell someone you love as much as I love her that you are dying? For over a year now, I have known that something was wrong, seriously wrong, and news of the worst came six months ago. ALS takes no prisoners and pulls those it snares to the depths of hell before the ultimate healing of the body can occur.

I write this today in hopes that the written word may help me summon the courage to, or gain insight as to how to, deliver the news of the black spot marking our time together. I have delayed, perhaps for selfish reasons, telling her what she has a right to know. It just seemed that there was always one more visit with our grandchildren, my fear of complicating her surgery, the promise of our forty-third anniversary on the San Antonio River, or another brief moment for the magic of the ranch. I hope she will forgive me. If I could only put into words what the gleam I saw in those brown eyes so long ago has meant to me. Perhaps then she would understand why I wanted to keep it alive if only for another moment in time. I hope she will find it in her heart to forgive me for letting this thing come between us.

But I know the clock is running. Soon I must talk with her. I pray to God for wisdom and for the courage to do what I must.

AUGUST 30, 2004

Today, in a motel room in a distant place, I told Veleda. I picked this place because I did not want this message to mar the memories of any of the special places in our lives. I cannot write more because there are no words descriptive of that moment.

1

SEPTEMBER 1, 2004

In all of my other fights in life, I had a chance to defend myself, to strike back, to land a punch. Even during our miserable 0-10 football season my senior year in high school, there was always the chance to hit a lick, to let them know you were on the field. During an injury- and strife-filled season, one night we ran twelve Round Rock High Dragons onto the field to face sixty-four Georgetown Eagles. For the twelve of us (we had twelve players because two brave souls had been recruited from study hall earlier that day), it was not a matter of our outscoring their high-powered offense. It was all about standing in the face of intimidation and refusing to admit you were whipped. The Eagles got a scrap that night, and we walked off the field with our dignity intact.

That is what makes this disease so hard to deal with. If there were just something I could do to show I will not go easily. If I could just land a punch, I would feel better. I've got to find a way.

SEPTEMBER 4, 2004

I went to the Woods because I wished to live deliberately, to front only the essential facts of life, and see if I could not learn what it had to teach, and not, when I came to die, discover that I had not lived...I wanted to live deeply and suck out all the marrow of life.—Henry David Thoreau[1]

In 1998 Veleda and I left academia for a new life on a Hill Country ranch. The life we had known was very good to us, but after thirty-five years there were other things we wanted to do. She left her university professorship in the English department and I left behind a college presidency. When I told the board of regents I wanted to pursue another life "while I could still put a saddle on a good horse," some of them looked at me as though I had just announced we were moving to Mongolia.

The place we were moving to was nowhere close to Mongolia, but the truth was it wasn't very close to anyplace. In between us and the nearest stoplight thirty-five miles away are at least seven miles of bone-jarring dirt road, which will make short work of all but the sturdiest vehicles. At the time we made the move, the nearest neighbor was two miles away. The only livable structure on the place was a four-room rock hunting cabin constructed during World War II.

It was at this place we decided to spend the rest of our time together. Some of our friends believed we had lost our minds, but what they did not know was that this was the only real home we had known together. Our career migration had taken us to many locations, but no place other than the ranch had the sense of permanency you could call a home. It was our family's place of memories, and there is history here. Veleda's family began ranching on this place 120 years ago, and my ancestors came to the county in the 1850s. There is no record they ever knew each other, but they were probably on different sides during a Mason County range war.

Over the years we have remodeled the house and added an addition and a guest house, built fences, cut cedar, planted native grasses, and established a good herd of black cattle. There is no exhaustion with this work, just exhilaration, for each day you see something evolve into a form that did not exist the day before.

No one can live here without being shaped by the land. There were lessons from the land we had forgotten, and there are those yet to be learned. It is much easier here, for there is so little clutter to contend with. We have found anew the special times that exist between daylight and dark when morning coffee and wine at sunset are savored amid the turning of the day. In this place we have become students again: students of nature, readers of good works, and contemplators of life's meaning. Here we know the depths of life that only shared work, shared pain, and shared hopes can bring together. As with John and Abigail Adams, we have looked out at the world together, and it has been wonderful.

SEPTEMBER 5, 2004

My left hand is beginning to fail me. Each day my grip weakens and the fine motor skills are about gone. My right hand is still strong though. Just like Santiago in Hemingway's *The Old Man and the Sea*, my right never fails me.[2] As long as the right stays alive I can still do my ranch work, and there is hope for some accomplishment. As long as the right stays with me, I can go on with life and people around me will not treat me like I am sick. I try to judge when my right will go by the rate of progression in the left. I would guess I have no more than a year.

September 8, 2004

Dear Jeff, Jennifer, Chad, Amy, Christian, Mariah, and Thomas,

By now you will have had some time to digest my phone message to you last week. I struggled for months with the question of when and how to talk with you about things. My only thought, perhaps selfish, was that I wanted to delay the message as long as possible. My doctors and Mom urged me to talk with the family, so for better or worse, I made the call last week.

Though I have been able to cope with the situation very well for the past six months, this week I have to say has been difficult. ALS is now our family's disease and the implications of that have not been easy for me. I am confident I will do better in time. I have always been inspired by God's message in Ecclesiastes, reminding us that for all things there is a time and a season. We sometimes have no choice as to what happens in life, but I do believe we always have a choice as to how we deal with what happens in life. For me, and for Mom, we chose to live well for as long as we can.

An interesting thing about casual conversation is that people will often say, "If I knew I was going to die, I would change my life and do so and so." Shortly before he died, Michael Landon said, "I wish they would tell us in the beginning that we are dying and then maybe we would start living." It's funny: Other than spending more time with you, there is nothing whatsoever that I want to change in my life. When the physician told me I had ALS, he said in the same breath, "I am sorry I can't explain why bad things happen to good people." My response to him was, "I really have no reason to complain; my life has been blessed and there are people around me who love me." I write this to say to each of you what a blessing you have been to me and how much I look forward to our time together in the future.

Speaking of the future, I do hope it will be possible for us to spend Christmas together this year. We have never been together as a family before, and it would be a nice gift for Mom and me if it can be arranged.

Shakespeare said, "It is an ill wind that blows no good."[3] Despite the way this story will in the end play itself out, there is some good that can come from it. I would hope that from the experience we will become closer as a family. Each of you has your unique beliefs that I respect (even though you sometimes vote for those disgusting Republicans) and each of you has special strengths. Most successful organizations and all great families are built on strengths. If we look for the good in other people we inevitably find it, and if we build on our strengths we are all the better for the effort. My great hope and my prayer each day is that we will share that road into the time ahead.

Finally, a word about Mom. She will have a much more difficult time than I in dealing with what we face. I urge your prayers for her and your every effort to make life for her as easy as possible.

My love to each of you,
Dad

September 15, 2004

The literature on ALS warns patients they will likely have episodes of unexplained crying, or in some cases, unexplained laughter. For six months there were no tears, but now there are powerful urges to cry at the least provocation. I mask it most of the time by avoiding emotional events or keeping my mind off of what is happening to me. When it is really bad, I cry silently in the night while she sleeps. It creeps through at other times. Memorable songs, family pictures, sunsets with Veleda by my side, all remind me of what I am about to lose. Sometimes we cry together. I guess I am having trouble dealing with this because crying is not something men readily do in my culture.

It is a part of that hard Texas crust that would best be scraped away.

OCTOBER 9, 2004

In a better time, I built a rock fence. With the dimming of this day, I sit on the front porch and study the interlaced wall of limestone that marks the western boundary of the yard. It could have been woven wire like those that intersect on the north and south, but I wanted a rock fence. Rock fences give character to the rugged Texas Hill Country and say something of those who came here in an earlier time.

An old rancher once told me that "a good rock man can build ten feet of fence a day." Though I had to haul the rock in from the pasture, I was confident I could complete the job in a couple of weeks. After a month of hauling rocks and painstakingly fitting them into place, it occurred to me that I had undertaken a substantial project. In the following month I came to truly appreciate the legacy of those who had passed this way before me. I now know something of the muscle ache and back pain that comes at the end of a day when you have hauled a half ton of rock in from the pasture. I have experienced the euphoria that comes from seeing something of my own hand rise up from the ground. The fence is my friend now. Though it stands between me and the setting sun, it speaks of hot August days, hard labor, smashed fingers, and satisfaction.

Unfortunately, too often today the measure of a career is an annuity check, which arrives each month at a house built by someone else, for a person who has nothing meaningful to do with the time that is left. I am grateful to God for the opportunity to have known more.

OCTOBER 10, 2004

We have just returned from a memorable trip to Germany to attend a family reunion of Veleda's German cousins. While there one evening, we had a delightful dinner in a quaint Black Forest tavern. During our meal, one of our party discovered an interesting quote from actress Claudia Cardinale on one of the restaurant coasters. Veleda's translation of the quote from German goes something like this: "A marriage works best when both remain a little bit single."

The women immediately took exception to the remark. Giving Ms. Cardinale the benefit of the doubt, I urged the ladies not to rush to judgment. My remark made matters worse, and now faced with my own indictment, I tried without much success to explain myself. I saw in Ms. Cardinale's comment a message for married people to be involved in a perpetual courtship. This message came through to me because, like some people with limited futures, I find myself feeling as though I am courting her again.

In those early days of courtship at Texas State when I came to love her, I wanted us to be together constantly. Following our parting at night on the steps of her dorm, my agony began and I immediately began manufacturing some plan that would create the illusion of an accidental meeting on campus the next day. I even broke with my long-standing tradition of never studying by meeting her in the library at night. She studied and I acted the part, but I was really thinking of her and the prospect of walking her back to the dorm. Despite those brief moments of ecstasy, I knew courtship meant we would eventually be separated by holidays, class schedules, and work schedules. In the times we shared I savored each moment, for I knew our time together was limited.

Today I have returned to those times in all that I do with her. There are no ordinary days or nights. Though the black cloud is always there when I awake in the mornings, the first thing I do is to reach and touch her, and the old feeling comes back. We try not to be separated during the day even if it means she works with me in the pasture. I find myself wanting to give her gifts or to build things she wants. She touches me when she passes my chair and we hold hands on the front porch. When we are in crowds, I see her look at me with her sparkling brown eyes, and the effect is the same as it was so long ago. This difficult time has caused our love to move to a level of intensity we could never have predicted. If marriage does work best "when both remain a little bit single," then perhaps we should never stop courting.

OCTOBER 24, 2004

I worked on a windmill today. I have always enjoyed working off the ground. As a construction worker long ago, I learned the higher you are in the air, the less likely you are to have bosses looking over your shoulder. In some environments today, employees who work down the hall from the leader might just as well be fifty feet in the air. Here employees spend their days in a "spiritual desert" when their work for the organization or as individuals is seldom affirmed, because those in charge are management aficionados but leadership illiterates.

It could be said that a person with ALS has no business on a tower thirty feet in the air. On the other hand, if you have the strength to get there, what better place for an ALS patient to be than on the top of a windmill? The view from a place you will likely never return to is always the best.

I was reminded today of an ethic that still prevails in the rural parts of the Texas Hill Country. Our neighbor, who lost her husband several years ago, called to say her water well was no longer pumping. Here, neighbors do not let neighbors go long without water. Three of us, two in their seventies and I in my sixties, gathered to work on the well. Nearby are the corrals and old dipping vats where the Brandenberger brothers and other neighbors over the years brought thousands of cattle to be worked and dipped. They were drawn together by mutual needs and a common interest in helping one another. It was the way of life here.

If you look for it, you still see evidence of little things that bond people together in this place. People still wave at each other when they pass on the country roads. They yield to faster traffic on the blacktops leading into town. In our community, when you meet someone on the street, they look you in the eye and they speak to you when you come by. It would seem to me that for leaders of countries, corporations, or families, the first lesson for leadership is to stay in touch with your people. There are lessons from an earlier time we ought not to forget.

Somehow, it's easier to perceive these lessons from a perspective atop a windmill.

November 1, 2004

We elect a new president tomorrow. Despite all the election-year rhetoric, I do not believe the Founding Fathers ever intended our government to be what it is today. I think a careful examination of the times will show that today we are more of a corporate state managed by professional politicians than a republic. Leadership is more about reelection and the preservation of political parties than it is about leading the American people to a better place. The four billion dollars spent on the election came largely from special interest groups who will claim their prize at the expense of good government and the best interest of the American people. Tomorrow night one of the parties will celebrate a victory won largely through negative campaigning and spin doctors who make the candidates seem to be something they are not.

One choice on the ballot is a professional politician with a ton of political baggage. His scattered, liberal voting record has proven to be easy fodder for a tightly focused conservative right that leaves no stone unturned. His carefully crafted, politically correct campaign would lead us to believe we can spend our way into happiness and security. Though he is intellectually superior to the venerable incumbent president, mainstream Americans cannot identify with him.

Our other choice is a man who has spent a lifetime capitalizing on his family's money and influence. By any measure, his administration has favored the rich and powerful while ignoring the country's frightful drift toward a bifurcated society. His people have done a masterful job in masking a deplorable record, and the election will likely turn on the September 11 fears he shamelessly exploits.

Both candidates' images are nothing but facades. Everything they do is carefully scripted by others to present an image appealing to the largest number of likely voters in swing states. We are bombarded continually by their mean-spirited, negative campaign ads, which in reality are more an indictment of the character of the accuser than the accused. Where are the leaders who once ran on their own records rather than on the short-comings of their opponents? Whatever happened to leaders who defy pollsters to give the right message to people who do not want to hear it? Where are the Abraham Lincolns, the Teddy Roosevelts, and the Harry Trumans of this world who stake their future on doing the right thing despite the political conse-quences? I was really proud of my first presidential vote, which went to Barry Goldwater, because he had the courage to cover the ground he stood on. I wish I had been old enough to vote for Harry Truman. Today most people like him and Goldwater are weeded out by the system.

Despite the abysmal leadership our parties provide, I take heart from a belief that the leadership that has the most pro-found effect on our country does not necessarily come from Pennsylvania Avenue in Washington, DC, but in reality it evolves from Main Street in the USA. Here, you are most likely to find leaders who seek the greater good for those they serve. It is in this place that lessons abound for all who seek to become authentic leaders.

Chapter 1
Leaders Worth Following

What is there about some leaders that causes others to want to follow them into the unknown? Why are followers willing to support, defend, and nurture some leaders, while other leaders contend with environments filled with sabotage, mutiny, and betrayal? Intelligent people in all quality environments never follow blindly, but they do give their time, energy, and emotional support to leaders they believe are taking them to a better place.

What sets apart leaders who lead well from those who do not? This question first intrigued me long ago when, as a college dean, I had an opportunity to interact with leadership teams from 106 public school campuses. The Effective Schools Project (ESP) at Tarleton State University was designed to partner our university with campus leadership teams consisting of principals and representative teachers. Our university professors regularly visited each of the participating campuses, where we served as consultants and became students of real-life issues affecting the public schools. The school campus teams also came to the university campus several times a year for leadership seminars conducted by nationally acclaimed speakers. The ESP received national recognition in 1992 when it was named an exemplary program by the National Council of States for In-Service Education, and it recently celebrated its twenty-fifth anniversary.

As I made my public school visits, I was immediately struck by the fact that, on some campuses, the staff was dedicated to the principal and worked diligently to support him or her in pursuit of campus goals. The message came through loud and clear; the staff wanted the principal to succeed and they were willing to commit themselves to that endeavor.

On a few campuses, though, the leadership climate was far from positive. The staff was not committed to seeing leadership succeed, and in some cases the school was filled with deceptive efforts to force the principal out. It was not uncommon on these campuses for a dramatic shift of allegiance to turn a charismatic teacher into the real campus leader.

Given this setting, I began to compare effective leaders to those who were less effective. I thought that surely the difference between the two groups could be found by looking at variables associated with the leaders' degrees, experience, age, gender, and school demographics. When all was said and done, no clear picture emerged. Other than a minor correlation associated with the experience of effective leaders, I could find no clue to the difference between the two groups of leaders. Over time, I regularly returned to study this mystery, but my conventional thinking was getting me nowhere.

A few years later when I stumbled onto the work of Robert Greenleaf, I believe I found the answer to my question. For many years Greenleaf was the director of management evaluation and research at AT&T. After an acclaimed career linked with the preparation and evaluation of hundreds of leaders at AT&T, he too began to ask, "Why are some corporate executives significantly more effective leaders than are others in the organization?" His simple, yet so powerful, conclusion has the potential to transform families, corporations, governments, and private entities: One element of leadership applies in all settings where leaders seek to impact the lives of others.[1]

Greenleaf was convinced that leaders of substance are people whose primary motivation is a deep desire to serve. He believed leaders worth following are actually viewed as "servants" by their followers. These servant leaders are empowered to lead by those around them because they believe leadership is more a way of living than a management strategy. Whether the leader is called Mom/Dad, supervisor, pastor, superintendent, CEO, or president, the principle remains the same. Regardless of the leader's title and rank, others in the organization will eventually make a conscious choice to authorize or deauthorize the leader.

No doubt history has been shaped by great men and women. Their mark on history, however, came not so much from what they did individually but from what they inspired others around them to do. Usually these leaders are affirmed by those about them because the choices leaders make benefit others when an otherwise different choice would benefit only the leader. Servant leaders are authorized to lead because others in the organization know they can trust them to make decisions for the greater good of the organization. In this environment, followers will usually passionately defend leadership and give of themselves to help leadership move the organization forward.

We tend to deauthorize leaders who are seen to be working for their own self-interest at the expense of the organization. Efforts by leaders to camouflage arrogance, greed, selfishness, and blind ambition are no more successful around the corporate table than they are around the family dinner table. People will eventually see them for what they are and, one way or another, resentment sets in, resulting in what I term deauthorization. Deauthorization may take the form of outright mutiny, as was the case with the Enron Corporation, or it may mean there will be a passionless compliance with leadership directives in hopes that a better day and new leadership will come. In either case, the unauthorized leaders never build great families, organizations, or countries.

Yes, I know some individuals who have shaped world history were far from being servant leaders. There are indeed individuals alive and well today leading organizations who have little or no regard for the needs of followers. In fact, there is probably a good leadership book waiting to be written entitled *Why Do Good Things Happen to Bad Leaders?* Inept leaders get to the top in various ways. Some people are at the right place at the right time, and others may manipulate the system to their advantage while ruthlessly eliminating rivals on their way to the top. These individuals may succeed in their quest to attract followers and reach their goal, but there is faint hope they will be remembered as effective leaders. Undoubtedly Adolf Hitler, Joseph Stalin, and Saddam Hussein were successful in their quest to lead nations, but they left pathetic legacies as dictators instead of as leaders. Leaders worth following are successful in gaining support from followers, and as with Abraham Lincoln,

Rosa Parks, Jimmy Carter, Martin Luther King, and Mahatma Gandhi, *they leave enduring legacies of service to others.*

This message does not mean that prestige and material rewards are unimportant. It just means that leadership is operating at a higher level of thinking. Jim Kouzes, author of *The Leadership Challenge*, once told me that servant leadership does not necessarily mean that leaders are serving the needs of followers, or that followers are serving the needs of the leadership; it means that they are all serving the greater good of the organization. World-class corporations like TD Industries, Southwest Airlines, and the Synovus Financial Corporation have all sought to find the path to the greater good through servant leadership. The profits of these corporations have repeatedly been above industry averages and each company is among the top tier of the Fortune list of "100 Best Companies to Work For in America." When servant leadership becomes the cornerstone of thinking within an organization, the financial, emotional, and commitment dividends are likely to improve.[2]

In the leadership seminars I have conducted around the country, individuals often ask, "Is servant leadership the new model for leading organizations?" The answer to this question is decidedly no. I say this first of all because servant leadership is not new. The basic concepts have been with us for two thousand years. Servant leadership is also not a leadership model because models are based on processes. I believe in some process models such as Total Quality Management and the DuPont Model because they have been helpful in leading organizations forward. Process models, however, tend to focus on systems and procedures, not on individuals. When individuals do come into play in process models, it is generally through systems for dealing with all those people in the organization who "need to be fixed." There are indeed people in organizations whose behavior needs to be changed because they hinder progress and make the lives of co-workers miserable. Anyone who has held a management position can quickly suggest names for the "needs to be fixed" list.

The unique thing about servant leadership is that it does not focus on all those other people out there who need to be changed. It focuses on the only person in this world we have control over, and that is the person we see in the mirror each morning. Leadership legacies are not so much carefully crafted blueprints for an orderly life as they are chronicles of how we respond to people and situations. We have no choice as to when our defining moments in life will come, but we do have a choice as to how we will respond in those moments. The meaningful messages in life, messages that affirm the worth of those around us, messages that prove we are worthy of trust, messages that demonstrate we have courage under fire, are communicated in those moments.

Our society places a high value on intelligence, energy, vision, charisma, and, sometimes, good looks as attributes of leadership. While these attributes are important and some people ride them to high places in the organization, they will not alone ensure success. In today's complex world, no leader, regardless of intellect, can know all there is to know about how to manage ever-changing organizations.

One example of the proliferation of information leaders must stay on top of can be seen in the field of medicine. In 1990 a researcher estimated the number of indexed articles in medical journals to be six hundred thousand. Given the ever-increasing number of articles produced each year, if a physician set out to survey the literature by reading two articles per day for twelve months he would, at the end of one year, be eight hundred years further behind than when he started.[3] I have known some outstanding physicians, but I do not believe any of them can know all there is to know about their field. When they restore critically ill patients back to good health, they do so through the efforts of many people with differing expertise.

The same principle applies to those who lead organizations. Dr. John Horn, the legendary former superintendent of schools in Mesquite, Texas, once told me, "The only way a leader is going to succeed is through relationships." In this complex world, none of us is really bright enough to know all we need to know about leadership, nor are there enough hours in the day to do all that we feel needs to be done. We will succeed as leaders only if we accept our dependence on others and if a lot of other people want us to succeed. The number of one-to-one relationships is a pretty good predictor of success for most leaders.

Leaders worth following know that what they are about is bigger than they are.[4] I have worked as a consultant to a number of troubled organizations over the years. In this role, you quickly learn that there are some obstacles that are particularly difficult to overcome. One of the most problematic situations is when an attitude prevails among some top leaders that leadership is "all about me" rather than "all about those I seek to lead." In talking with top management, you can usually tell in the first few moments what the organization's leadership values are. When the conversation is peppered with "I" as opposed to "we," I know the road ahead will be long and difficult. In these organizations, leadership behavior is akin to that of NFL running backs who prance and dance in the end zone or linebackers who run toward the TV cameras rather than accepting the congratulations of teammates. In either case, these individuals ignore the fact that they were in a position to shine because ten other players were carrying out their own responsibilities.

Evidence of those who lead well, seeing the greater good, can be found in Jim Collins's study of 1,435 successful corporations.[5] From this group Collins sought to identify the companies in which transitions occurred that moved them from good to great performance. In this case, the great companies were defined in part as companies where transitions occurred that resulted in cumulative stock returns of at least three times the general stock market for a period of fifteen years. With this benchmark in place, the list was quickly shortened from 1,435 to 11 companies. The study then began to investigate what caused the companies to move from good to great and in particular what role, if any, leadership had in the transformation. Traditional thinking would suggest that the leaders in the great companies would be larger-than-life stereotypes with enormous egos and a flair for dramatics. What they found was a different kind of leader. The data revealed that the eleven CEOs had only two common characteristics.

First, they were known for their humbleness. Whenever they were asked about their success, they were quick to give credit to those around them. They regularly talked about how lucky they were to work with such talented people. They never saw the success of the company as an extension of their own personalities.

As the Civil War progressed, Abraham Lincoln became the focal point of vicious criticism from both inside and outside his party. One of the president's more vociferous critics was cabinet member Edwin Stanton. In an interview with the press, Stanton was once reported to say about Lincoln, "He looks like a baboon."[6] When asked about Stanton's uncomplimentary comment, Lincoln said, "Well it must be true because Secretary Stanton is a mighty smart man." It was Edwin Stanton who later grieved at the bedside of the mortally wounded Lincoln. When Lincoln's life slipped away, Stanton announced to the world: "He now belongs to the ages."[7] Some would say Lincoln's humbleness spawned a magnanimous spirit and his most enduring legacy.

Second, Collins found that the great leaders were known by their unrelenting personal will. Once the mission of the company was identified, the leaders began an inexorable march to excellence. They refused to be sidetracked or taken off course by failures or by those who lacked the courage or stamina to stand under fire.[8]

The life of wartime president Harry Truman could hardly be described in terms of straight-line ascendancy to the presidency. His life, into middle age, was characterized by repeated failures. As a frail and weak child, he could not please a demanding father. He was an unsuccessful farmer and he failed in more than one business venture. It took an eight-year courtship for him to convince his future wife, Bess, that he was a worthy candidate for marriage. When elected to the U.S. Senate from Missouri, he was shunned by Senate colleagues because of his association with the Pendergast political machine, known for its dirty dealings, in Kansas City. Truman never blamed others for his problems, but from each bad experience a tougher, more resilient man emerged.[9]

When he was suddenly thrust into the presidency by the death of Franklin Roosevelt, many feared the worst for the country. Some thought the office of vice president had become a mere ornament in the Roosevelt presidency. All of the other vice presidents who served Roosevelt ran afoul of the president's wishes and were discarded. Most importantly, FDR had not kept Truman apprised of the nation's war plans, including the development of the atomic bomb. He would soon have to deal with the postwar ambitions of Winston Churchill and Joseph Stalin and the election of a Republican Congress. Contrary to the belief that he would fold under pressure, Truman seemed to thrive in the heat of battle. In Washington he told friends and foes alike, "If you can't stand the heat, get out of the kitchen." He challenged the nation, he challenged Congress, and he challenged himself to bring the earliest possible end to the war. He went about his task with an incredible vigor and with the characteristic stubborn will for which his home state was known. His decision to use the atomic bomb on Hiroshima and Nagasaki is still debated by historians, but Truman would later say he never thought twice about the decision.

Of all Truman's battles, perhaps the election of 1948 best exemplified his unrelenting will. Practically no one in the country, including most members of his own political party, believed he had a chance to win the election. Political confidants told him that if he continued to press his Civil Rights agenda, he probably would not even receive the party's nomination. He responded by telling them that for him, the issue was worth losing the nomination.[10]

Truman refused to capitulate to the naysayers. He began his whistle-stop tour of the country by appealing to the middle class and mainstream America. He sometimes made sixteen speeches a day detailing his populist agenda. Historian David McCullough would later say that what Truman told the American people was, "Here I am, here's what I stand for— here's what I'm going to do if you keep me in the job. You decide."[11] Few people, and in particular the pollsters, understood that this was the real message America wanted to hear. On Election Day Truman startled the world, the nation, and his mother-in-law by soundly defeating Thomas Dewey.

Leaders worth following are not genetic accidents; they are people who understand that how they manage themselves largely determines the degree to which followers will authorize them to lead. They also understand that the most important instrument in any orchestra is the second fiddle, because it is the second fiddles that create the harmony.[12]

November 18, 2004

In his book *It's Not about the Bike*, Lance Armstrong tells the story of his remarkable battle with testicular cancer. He began his fight knowing there was a 90 percent chance he was going to lose. He not only survived, but as the world now knows, he went on to claim his place as one of the great cyclists in history. While reading his book, I was struck by one of its powerful messages, and I have used the following quote in seminars around the country: "If children have the ability to ignore odds and percentages, then maybe we can learn from them."[13]

Children do not understand percentages, but they do believe in hope. They cannot comprehend the realities of science, but they do believe in possibilities. Like a child, Lance Armstrong ignored the odds, staked his future on hope, and won.

Where do you find hope when your doctors all say you are going to die? I struggle with that because I do not believe in giving up on hope. I look for hope each day, but it is not like before. My hope now is that I will have the courage to face this thing with dignity. My hope today is that I will be able to look beyond myself to the beauty in this world. I am surrounded by the love of my family and I hope I can show them what it means to me. I have learned that hope will always be there; you just have to look in the right places.

November 22, 2004

I stopped taking Rilutek two days ago, and I feel dramatically better. The drug has proven to be effective in extending the lives of some ALS patients by a few months, but from the moment I began taking it, the side effects made life miserable. Whatever it has to offer, the drug has been taking more from me than it can give. I would much rather have some quality moments with my family than whatever existence Rilutek might provide me in the long run. Veleda and I had wine on the front porch this evening while the sun disappeared behind Cannon Mountain.

NOVEMBER 22, 2004

Sometimes in the night I think about earlier times and another life. I spent all of my youth in small towns, but I hardly had a Beaver Cleaver existence.

My earliest memories are of a tranquil life on our ranch in Central Texas. My dad, having lived through a depression following a great war, was convinced another would follow. Fearful of the mortgage the bank held on land he'd earlier purchased for fifteen dollars an acre, he sold out when offered a ten-dollar-per-acre profit. He moved the family to a ninety-acre farm near the small town of Bertram, forty miles north of Austin.

My dad was a jack-of-all-trades. He literally rode out the Great Depression on freight trains as he and other hobos traveled from place to place looking for work. He spent some time in the oil patch, worked in construction, and came to be an excellent chef while cooking in the Civilian Conservation Corps. One Depression story he told me had him dead broke in Tennessee and longing to be home in Texas. In the "village," as he described the place where his fellow travelers congregated near the tracks, someone offered him a whetrock and twenty-five cents in exchange for his golf cap. That night, hatless and with a ten-cent loaf of bread and a fifteen-cent jar of peanut butter in his knapsack, he caught a westbound train. A few days later, very tired of peanut butter, he made it home. Today the whetrock is one of my prized possessions.

We moved to Bertram, Texas, two days before I was to begin first grade. In those days there was no kindergarten for rural kids, so I had never been in a schoolhouse before. I vividly remember our driving up to the campus the day school began and my mother telling me to "go on up to the schoolhouse." I watched her drive off, then turned and began one of the longest walks in my life. Because we lived so far from town, I had seldom been around other children. The campus was filled with children, all of whom seemed to know one another. They stared but did not speak as I walked by. One person on campus I did know was my cousin Molly. I immediately latched on to her and became her shadow. In a few days she began to tire of my constant presence and went off to play with some of the other girls. I felt even more alone.

Fortunately for me, our teacher was Miss Selma Johnson. She would prove to be one of the dearest people I have ever known. I spent a lot of time on her lap. I still miss her hugs today.

While my formal education was under way at the public school, another kind of education was about to begin. Not long after school began, my dad opened a pool hall in town and a few months later he also began to operate the Friendly Café. He did most of the cooking and my mother waited on tables. I ran the streets.

When school ended, I walked to the café and stayed there until we closed each night at 10:00 p.m. Mother helped me with my lessons in between waiting on tables; then I was pretty well on my own until closing time. In lieu of a babysitter, my folks let me go to the picture show several nights a week. In those days it did not seem out of the ordinary for a seven-year-old to go alone to the movie theater at night. The Globe Theater was only three blocks from the café, so I was never really that far away. The trip back to the café, though, meant I had to pass the dark alleyway between Ottinger's General Store and Webb Grocery. I developed several strategies for getting past this place, which I feared was filled with every kind of evil. One approach was to wait until teens on dates came along on their way to the café for a Coke. Uninvited, I would join them until we reached safety on the other side. On most school nights, though, I could not depend on the availability of an escort, so I had to improvise. If the movie that night was a murder mystery or a monster show, I would run down the middle of the street from the drugstore to Newton's service station, where the light was better. Later, when I got my Western Flyer bike, neither man nor beast had a chance of catching me.

The period just after the close of World War II was an exciting time in Bertram, Texas. America's greatest generation had come home from war. Most who returned to their hometown did not know then that the agrarian society that produced them was about to disappear. They came back to their place of birth to search for work, wives, and a return to normalcy. Most had discharge money in their pockets and some had demons in their minds.

On Saturday nights at the pool hall and on the streets, I saw what the war had done to some of them. One vet who returned from the Pacific, with memories he probably never shared, would scream in the middle of the picture show. Once when some older boys set off firecrackers in the street, I saw a shell-shocked man fall to the ground; for several minutes afterward he shook uncontrollably. In groups of two or three, they would sit in parked cars and drink whiskey until the bottle was empty or sleep overcame them. These men liked me. Why, I will never know, because I was an obnoxious little devil. They gave me nickels, nicknamed me Curley (for my bur haircut), and teased me unmercifully. Though I was far from innocent, I think they saw something in me they had lost. The war had taken them across a bridge from which there was no return.

I pretty well had the run of the town, but a few places were strictly off limits, and I knew my parents had better not see me at any of them. One was the old abandoned gin mill, filled with all kinds of equipment, some of which were two stories tall. Its darkened corners and lofty perches made it a fabulous place for playing army and hide-and-seek. The other forbidden place I could not stay away from was the railroad. At that time, the train stopped on summer days to pick up cotton bales stacked on the platform by the depot. Beneath the platform, we could spy on the train crew and see up close the huge steam engine that belched fire and steam. At that place long ago, my great-grandfather Taylor had won a fifty-dollar bet by strapping a five-hundred-pound bale of cotton onto his back and carrying it across the platform.

Lanny Ross and I were playing west of the platform one day when a train came around the curve on its way to Austin. I had sold some "sodie water bottles" that morning for two cents each, so I had some pennies in my pocket. Lanny suggested we put one of the pennies on the track in the path of the oncoming train. Perhaps because I was already in forbidden territory, I could not resist such a daring act. We put the penny on the track and hid ourselves in a ditch to watch what would happen. Our plan would have worked without a hitch had not Morris McDaniel appeared on the scene. We yelled for him to join us in the ditch, where we told him about our sinister plans. By this time the train was bearing down on the penny at a high rate of speed. Morris was older and wiser than us, so we believed him when he told us the penny "would surely derail the train engine." By that time it was too late to beat the train to the penny, so I stood there in absolute horror and watched the train race toward its impending doom—and my eternal damnation.

Not long after the train incident, Lanny and I decided to ride his horse, Dusty. Dusty never really appreciated the image of "Lanny the mounted warrior" that I hoped to project. In fact, she spent a great deal of her time avoiding capture, but on this day she succumbed to the lure of the shelled corn we put in her pen. Since we were not much more than stirrup-high, it was with great difficulty that we got the saddle in place.

We set off into the pasture with Lanny in the saddle and me riding behind. Sometime during the ride, we began talking about how movie cowboys on the run would cover their trail by dragging brush behind them. As fate would have it, we soon passed a pile of brush that caught our attention. Lanny untied his nylon parachute rope and we looped it around one of the limbs in the brush pile. Lanny tied the rope to the saddle horn and pointed Dusty up the trail. As we moved forward, our tree limb, as well as the entire brush pile around it, was set in motion. The strange noise behind her immediately put Dusty into a dead run. We soon realized there was no stopping her, for the faster she ran, the faster whatever it was that chased her ran. The fact that Lanny was all I had to hold on to was not particularly reassuring, for all he seemed to be able to say, in a very subdued spirit, was "Whoa, Dusty, whoa."

Ahead on the trail we could see overhanging limbs. Lanny dodged to the left and I to the right. Eventually the trail made a short turn to the left and it was at this point that we became airborne. Lanny hit the ground first and I landed on top of him. Somewhere in the distance we could hear the thrashing of brush, but we both spent the next several minutes sucking air back into our lungs. I am sure we were not the first cowboys to walk home, but it seemed like it at the time. At the corral we found Dusty standing there waiting for more corn. The parachute rope remained attached to the saddle on one end and on the other was a live-oak branch, which at one time had been a brush pile.

If the truth were known, Lanny and I got into a great deal of mischief. Our families both moved from Bertram when we were in high school, and I saw only a little of him after that. Lanny moved on to Austin where I was told he began to run with a rather rough crowd. I didn't hear anything about him again until I learned he had been sentenced to thirty years in the penitentiary.

Some said he was unfairly convicted. Every time I think of him, though, I am reminded that we have two legal systems in the United States. One system is for the likes of O. J. Simpson, Cullen Davis, and Michael Jackson, with another system for Lanny and the rest of us. Shortly before his release, I reopened our acquaintanceship. We exchanged letters and made plans to get together when he was released. He had become a renowned saddlemaker while in prison, and I made contact with some people in the industry about giving him a job. He was released a few days before Christmas in 2004, and while celebrating his first Christmas Eve with family in thirty years, he died of a heart attack. I regret that we never had the opportunity to visit again and talk about the times when we terrorized the railroad tracks in Bertram.

By today's standards, some would say I was a neglected child. If that were true, I never knew it. In addition to my parents, I had a dozen or so aunts and uncles in the community who inevitably learned about my mischievous acts, for there were no lasting secrets in Bertram. In a way, I would have to say that the entire community looked after me. I knew if I acted up in the picture show, the proprietor, Doss Smith, would quickly read me the riot act. Had I not been able to outrun him, Bob Brewer would surely have paddled my rear end for running with abandon through his mercantile store. Even the World War II veterans who caroused in the streets on Saturday nights looked after me. Yes, sometimes they put me up to mischievous pranks, but on more than one occasion I felt a firm hand on my shoulder and a gentle nudge toward a corrected course. In all those early years on the streets, I never once felt threatened by another human being. Whenever I think back to happy moments in my youth, my thoughts inevitably settle on Bertram.

NOVEMBER 23, 2004

Most nights she wants to massage my left arm before we go to bed. I tell her the problem is not in my arm but in my brain. I think we both know my arm is the first part of me to die, but she persists as though she could somehow rub life back into it. In a world of uncertainty, she is certainty. I am told a grave marker somewhere says, "If the love of my family could have saved me, I would still be alive." When I think about those who die never knowing the kind of love my family has given me, I realize how truly blessed I have been.

DECEMBER 6, 2004

I have experienced two kinds of mind-enhancing experiences in my lifetime. The first was the birth of our children. The moment Jeff, and later Chad, arrived, my perception of the world changed because I began to see through their eyes. Nothing is simple or mundane in the eyes of a child. Unlike adults, whose life experiences often lead them to be calloused and cynical, children see the world with a sense of wonder. I am amazed at how the boys could find human drama in the most unlikely places; even in an environment desecrated by commercial interests, they saw beauty wherever we went. I wanted to teach them about nature, music, books, and sports, but I was likely the real learner.

The second mind-enhancing experience came when I was writing my novel. Just as with the birth of our children, the venture into fiction opened my eyes to things I have never seen before. I believe writers feed more on what they see in others than what they find in themselves. Everyone I met became a quick study for some distinguishing characteristic that might set him or her apart as one of the characters in the book. I came to see mannerisms, eccentricities, strengths, and weaknesses in a light I had not known before. Veleda says writers spend too much of their time observing and not enough time participating in life. Given the track record of many novelists, I suspect she is right, but I have felt ever so briefly the opiate that compels them.

To my great pleasure, I am now having a third mind-enhancing experience. To know there is a limited amount of time to see anything changes your mind about how you see everything. The dark cloud is still there, but I see everything now with an intensity I never imagined possible. Nothing now is ordinary.

JANUARY 30, 2005

Sometimes in the past I wondered how my faith in God would be affected should I learn that I had a life-threatening disease. The answer to that question has slowly come to me over the past several months. My faith has not lessened; in fact, it has been strengthened by this experience. The time I spend each day in prayer and meditation has had a remarkable cleansing effect on the clutter that once occupied my mind.

I cannot bring myself to ask God to heal me because I do not know the nature of his plans; I matter so little in the grand scheme of the universe. I do ask for courage and the will to fight this disease. In that regard I am comforted, and I now see each day with a renewed purpose that I did not feel in the beginning.

The greatest challenge to my faith has not been this disease; rather it comes from what I see being done in the name of religion. The more religions become institutionalized, the less tolerant they are, and the more they create a God in their own image. I cannot imagine a God of love being pleased with a world where people of faith are consumed with the needs of the moment, ignorant of the broad view the great teachers taught us, and driven by zeal to obliterate all who do not share their own narrow beliefs.

FEBRUARY 3, 2005

A friend of mine once accepted a high school principalship in a school with many problems. In the preceding year, the campus had been ravaged by vandalism, fights, drug abuse, and racial strife. Most of the teachers who worked on that campus dreaded the start of the new school year and, in particular, the opening-day assembly. This event was characterized by disorderly conduct, catcalls, and a general disrespect for school authorities.

As he began his new assignment, though, Jack believed the school could do better. His teachers were skeptical when he announced that there would be an opening-day assembly, including the singing of the "Star-Spangled Banner" and a pledge to the flag. They were shocked when he told his staff he intended to have the local radio station present to broadcast the proceedings. The teachers expected the worst. The assembly began just as the teachers had feared. The students were disruptive and disrespectful to the new principal.

To everyone's shock, Jack immediately stopped the assembly and, pointing to disruptive students, had each of them removed from the auditorium by school authorities. A strange silence akin to attentiveness began to settle over the audience, but it didn't last long. When the audience was asked to stand and sing the national anthem, some students began to act out again. To everyone's surprise, Jack came back to the mike and told the audience to stop singing. He then relayed to those assembled, and by this time to an intensely interested radio audience, that they would stay there all day until proper respect was shown for the national anthem. When he stopped the singing of the national anthem for the second time, people began to realize that he was serious. When the assembly ended, students, faculty, and parents realized that for their school, a new day had begun and that there was a good chance a productive academic year was about to begin.

There was no doubt among any of those who knew Jack that he had a commanding presence. He was never arrogant or condescending, but you always knew on which side of the line he stood. He had high expectations for himself and everyone around him in the organization, and he was convinced good things were going to happen at the school. When students and teachers came to accept his enthusiasm and respect his grit, a major transformation began to unfold.

Chapter 2
The Power of Presence

Courage is not the absence of fear; rather it is the ability to take action in the face of fear.—Nancy Anderson[1]

Leadership *presence* is the one indisputable attribute that all effective leaders possess. Presence is difficult to explain and hard to describe, but is easily recognizable in great leaders. Those who have it are trusted by followers, and they can lead organizations to great heights. Leaders who have no sense of presence tend to create anxiety-ridden organizations incapable of thinking beyond the crisis of the moment.

Ask any CEO, father, mother, army general, or shop foreman what he or she worries about, and in short order they can give you a top ten list of forces out there with the capacity to seriously disrupt the organization. Some of these forces they have to contend with on a daily basis, and others are worst-case scenarios that may never happen but still have to play a part in a leader's thinking process. These tensions reflect current tensions in society, they represent complex issues, they will likely not go away, and they sometimes lead to dysfunctional organizations. The leader's presence has a huge influence on the degree to which unhealthy, sometimes sinister, influences become invasive forces within the organization.

By the summer of 1940 as World War II began in earnest, the Nazi war machine raced across Eastern Europe. In a few months the Germans claimed more strategic territory than they did in all of the Great War. Poland, Denmark, and France were quickly forced into submission, and Great Britain was on the verge of defeat. The remnants of the British army had been pushed into the sea at Dunkirk, and only a superhuman effort by Britishers manning every possible kind of floating craft would prevent their being obliterated by the Nazi blitzkrieg.

Much of London had been reduced to rubble by the Luftwaffe while most of its citizens lived nights of terror in subway caverns. So dismal were the prospects for Great Britain that some highly placed people in the United States were urging President Roosevelt to seek a separate peace with Germany.

In this bleak environment a portly senior citizen with a heart condition, who as a youth suffered from a speech impediment, who with the scorn of many was forced to resign as First Lord of the Admiralty in 1915, and who sometimes liked to drink too much brandy, stood up amid the London rubble. His message to freedom-loving people throughout the world that day was:

> We shall go on to the end, we shall fight in France, we shall fight on the seas and oceans, we shall fight with growing confidence and growing strength in the air, we shall defend our Island, whatever the cost may be, we shall fight on the beaches, we shall fight on the landing grounds, we shall fight in the fields and in the streets, we shall fight in the hills; we shall never surrender...[2]

Sir Winston Churchill's message was more than a statement of defiance toward the Nazis. It was a message of hope for his people. He was not acting out of arrogance, for he knew the inherent dangers posed by the Nazis. He realized something had to stand between his people and the external threat.

A few months after the September 11 attacks on the World Trade Center in New York City, I was asked to speak to the Manhattan Division of the American Cancer Society. The event took place over a two-day period. In private moments I was able to have meaningful conversations with many of the 545 attendees. I do not know what they learned from my presentation, but I do know I learned a great deal from them. They told stories of utter horror and destruction. They told stories of huge personal losses. They also told stories of incredible gallantry.

Up to that time I didn't know much about Mayor Rudy Giuliani, but all of that was about to change. The people there talked about the incredible impact he had on their lives in the days after the attack. In the midst of the smoke and ash, they saw more than a politician. Mayor Giuliani was there rendering aid, comforting families who had lost loved ones, and, above all, defiantly proclaiming that the city would not be intimidated by sinister forces. Rudy Giuliani's leadership presence nurtured a spirit that would rebuild more than buildings.

Mayor Giuliani's actions in New York contrast dramatically with those of Louisiana Governor Kathleen Babineaux Blanco's remarks following Hurricane Katrina's disastrous impact on New Orleans. Days after the hurricane came ashore, Governor Blanco was asked by NBC's Matt Lauer what it was like to try to reassure the people devastated by the storm. She tried to muster optimism, then circled back to despair, "You know, our people out there are so fearful. They're so worried…It's a nightmare."[3] What the governor said was probably an accurate description of the situation, but the people didn't need someone giving them a description of what they already knew. The message they needed was, "There is a way out of this, there is hope for a brighter day, and if we believe in ourselves, we can get there."

Not all of us will lead in the aftermath of national disasters, but leaders must function in tension-filled environments. Some examples of real stress factors in the life of corporate America can be found in foreign competition, governmental regulations, changing market conditions, energy costs, and sometimes mutiny and sabotage in the workplace. On a daily basis most families cope with the real stressors associated with making ends meet, contending with social pressure, managing carpools, and protecting children in an increasingly violent world. Sometimes these pressures overwhelm organizations and families. If you haven't had a crisis that will need a strong leadership presence, your time is coming.

Edwin Friedman in his marvelous book *A Failure of Nerve: Leadership in the Age of the Quick Fix*, describes the power of presence as analogous to electrical fields.[4] Through electrical transmission lines, mega-voltage currents rush toward businesses, schools, churches, family homes, and other structures. These currents have the potential to do major harm to all buildings, but before they enter, the voltages are stepped down to a manageable level by transformers. Good leaders with presence act as transformers, in that they reduce to a manageable level any tensions seeking to invade the organization.

When we think of leaders with presence, images of Hollywood matinee idols backing down the bad guys often come to mind. The truth is, presence has little to do with physical size, gender, or good looks. Nor does presence mean a leader is unafraid.

In his first inaugural address, Franklin D. Roosevelt told the nation that courage comes from "realizing there is something else more important than fear."[5] Most psychologists agree that the only person who is never afraid in a life-threatening situation is a lunatic. Some traits of leadership we see in individuals who have a strong sense of presence are as follows.

Leaders Believe There Is Life on the Other Side of the Crisis

Strong leaders can see beyond the anxieties of the moment to a time when the crisis will not be a factor. The moment we accept the notion that things cannot get better, we are whipped. As I think back on the various leadership crises I have faced, most of them passed with minimal damage to the organization. I could have done some things differently and had fewer scars, but things always got better when we focused on what *could* be.

As a nation we tend to remember George Washington's Revolutionary War contributions in terms of the leadership he provided at places like Yorktown, Trenton, and Princeton. No doubt these battles played mightily in the eventual outcome of the war. His most important contribution to the war, however, may not have been made on the battlefield but rather in his valiant efforts to preserve his demoralized army at Valley Forge. When his army established its winter quarters there in 1777, they did so under desperate circumstances. They did not have adequate provisions, munitions were short, and most of his men wore uniforms unsuitable for the cold winter they were about to face. So pathetic were the uniforms that Washington would later say, "you might have tracked the army from White Marsh to Valley Forge by the blood of their feet."[6]

In the next six months twenty-five hundred men in his army would die of sickness and exposure to the elements. Despite his regular pleas to Congress for provisions, very little help ever came. In reality Washington could do practically nothing about the abysmal situation at Valley Forge other than help his men cope with very difficult circumstances. He did this with an iron hand and an indomitable spirit. To keep his army focused on the future, he drilled them constantly. His constant point of reference was the coming spring offensive and the victories to come. At times he was ruthless in what he did to keep the army focused on his mission. He had no reservations about having deserters shot. Throughout the ordeal he used his enormous leadership presence to keep his troops focused on their common pursuit of liberty.

The Great Depression, which began in 1929, paralyzed the American economy and drove our country to the depths of despair. Herbert Hoover is remembered by many people as the president who could not bring the country out of the Great Depression, while his successor, Franklin Roosevelt, is often given credit for turning the economy around.

If the economic impetus generated by the beginning of World War II is removed from consideration, some economists now believe that Hoover, not Roosevelt, had the better plan for returning the country to long-term prosperity. Why then was Hoover turned out in favor of Roosevelt in 1932?[7] Roosevelt was not a person of extraordinary intelligence, but he exuded confidence. The essence of his campaign was "Happy days are here again," and it worked magic with the American public. People have to believe in the leader before they can believe in the message. Roosevelt's message was one of confidence in the future, and he captured the imagination of the nation.

They Know What They Stand for Before the Crisis Occurs

The midst of a crisis is not the time for leaders to begin formulating a philosophy about integrity, consistency, and the needs of followers. Presence is a way of living that those around leaders see in them on a day-to-day basis.

Over the years I have taken leadership groups to visit a firm that epitomizes this point. In the 1950s, Jack Lowe founded a small Dallas-based construction company, which eventually became a highly successful firm called TD Industries. TD Industries was one of the first companies in the United States to incorporate servant leadership into its management structure. As the company grew, Jack Lowe and his son, Jack Lowe Jr., spent significant time and resources building an organization based on mutual respect and trust. His employees were given opportunities to buy stock in the company and incentive programs were established in which employees profited when the company did well. Values that the company stood for were constant points of reference when decisions were made.

In the 1980s, the once-prosperous company was caught in a strong recession within the construction industry and faced the prospects of bankruptcy. Jack Lowe needed capital to keep the company afloat. Given the economic climate, his hopes for generating capital were slim. In time he called his employees together to talk through the prospects of bankruptcy. He told them he needed capital and that the only source of money the company could lay its hands on was the employees' retirement account. He asked the employees to consider reinvesting their retirement funds in the company.

For most companies, such a request would never have been received favorably by employees. This was not the case with TD Industries' employees because they knew Jack Lowe. Over the years he had fought the battles beside them, they had seen him operate under pressure, and they knew his commitment to the company was unshakable. Many times they had seen him make decisions that were best for the company when a different choice would have been best for Jack Lowe. Some of the senior employees nearing retirement decided to muster out of the company, but most of the employees told him to take the money. Today, TD Industries is a multimillion-dollar company, continuing to thrive in the highly competitive construction industry.[8]

Leaders Are Visible

Leaders with presence are found in the middle of the fray. An interesting story involving leadership presence evolved from the battle of Waterloo in 1814. In the most decisive battle of his career, Napoleon marched onto the field of battle with more troops and superior artillery than those of his opponent, England's Duke of Wellington. Most historians say Napoleon was a military genius and should have won this pivotal battle in European history. A number of factors came into play that day, all of which resulted in Napoleon's defeat, and ultimately his demise.

Throughout the course of the battle, Napoleon remained with his general staff, largely unseen by the French troops in the field. Wellington, on the other hand, was at the front challenging and encouraging the British and allied soldiers. As long as Wellington could be seen standing, his troops knew there was hope for a victory. Napoleon had no physical presence on the battlefield that day, leaving his troops in confusion and subject to the herd mentality that often occurs in the absence of leadership. World history turned on the outcome of the battle and many believe Wellington's presence on the front lines was a major factor in Napoleon's defeat.[9]

All leaders inevitably have to make some unpopular decisions. In doing so they may quickly discover that "it can be lonely at the top." For example, the smiles are gone when you meet certain people in the hallway; small groups actively engaged in conversation become quiet when you come into the room; all at once it seems that after work some people have pressing business to discuss in the parking lot.

The leader's temptation may be to retreat into the safe confines of the office. If so, he or she is headed in the wrong direction. If there is difficulty in the organization, on the battlefield, or around the family supper table, the leader needs to be visible. If the leader is away from the action, naysayers are emboldened, communication breaks down, and hope fades.

Leaders Have a Challenging Presence

Leaders with presence challenge everyone in the organization to higher levels of performance. They are known by their unrelenting personal will, and they have high expectations of those around them. A challenging presence does not mean the leader is autocratic or authoritarian, but he or she may be seen that way by people in the organization who fail to meet their responsibilities.

Leaders with a challenging presence are not concerned about how they measure up in popularity contests; their greater concern is for the welfare of the organization. General George S. Patton Jr. is a classic example of a leader with a challenging presence. He was often maligned by a hostile press that implied that the troops of "Old Blood and Guts" suffered needless casualties and that he cared little about his men.

In truth, Patton was a very poor politician, but the evidence supports the fact that he was an excellent general. His casualty rate on the field of battle was significantly less than those who commanded similar forces in the European theater.[10] His commanding presence and his constant visibility on the front lines inspired incredible performances by those under his command.

Ultimately, presence comes from our inner being. The previously mentioned examples from history illustrate the power that leadership presence has to touch the spirit of nations. There is no guarantee it will ensure our triumph in a crisis, but in difficult circumstances, it may be the only resource we have.[11]

FEBRUARY 27, 2005

The Academy Awards will be presented tonight. As she has done for decades, Veleda will ignore my scorn for the event and will watch the program alone, long past the time I am in bed. I tell her she has too much class to be spending her time watching such a disingenuous event, but the power of fashion, glamour, and theatrics are too enticing. Yes, there have been extraordinary actors with enormous talent whose performances have and will be landmarks in our country's history. They deserve the attention and the financial rewards bestowed upon them by society.

The people seen coming down the red carpet tonight are not necessarily national treasures. We are a nation consumed with the glitz of popular culture. I cannot imagine why we are so enamored with silicone- and Botox-enhanced people who spend their time acting like they are someone they are not. No one looks like they do, and if you were to hose them down, they wouldn't look that way either.

If history is a great teacher, then the first lesson to be learned is that enduring civilizations are known by their heroes. From the Greeks we learned that the first order in society should be occupied by great thinkers. It is a sad state of affairs when people like Madonna and Mike Tyson are today household names, yet most of our citizens cannot list the names of one American who has won the Nobel Prize or a Pulitzer. As a nation we have produced authentic heroes by the score, yet the memory of them too often pales in the wake of pop icons who dominate the media in our youth-oriented society. This happens in all societies that lose their center and allow others to define their values for them.

FEBRUARY 28, 2005

So much for pride and making a stand against glitz. I curled up under a blanket with her last night and watched the Academy Awards from start to finish. I do not want to spend a part of any night separated.

MARCH 18, 2005

Someday we will have the answer to what causes ALS. Who knows what it will be, but the best guess of most researchers today is that it is likely caused, or strongly influenced by, the neurotoxins in the environment. In the name of maintaining a strong economy, we lead the world in spewing these poisons into streams, oceans, and the atmosphere. Neurotoxins affect the lives of all people, but they are particularly hazardous for children. Election years usually stir up some rhetoric about cleaning up these hazards, but children do not have as much power in Congress as do corporations.

Regardless of whatever caused me to have ALS, I know I set the stage for it myself. I did that by living an adrenalin-rushed life for too many years. Too often in the name of reaching a goal or completing another project, I ignored the messages my body tried to send me. Only in my last years as a college president, when I became interested in servant leadership, did I come to understand that a meaningful life is not really a wild assault, but a search for harmony within the elements. By then I think it was too late. The forces of destruction were already at play within my body.

Though the message from most of my doctors is that I cannot survive, I believe the body has the ability to heal itself from any disease. One of my doctors believes this as well, and he refuses to talk with me about anything but living. He has taught me to first move away from thinking "I must fight this thing" or that "I cannot defeat this thing," and to accept the fact that I have ALS and that within my body are healing powers that can combat this disease. How those powers are activated, whether through prayer, lifestyle changes, deactivation of my adrenaline rushes, or a nontoxic diet, I do not know. I understand that time and the vicious nature of this disease are working against me, but if I can venture far enough into the depths, I may find the healing waters.

APRIL 22, 2005

Recently at an ALS clinic, I sat in a hospital lobby with a number of patients in various stages of decline. I had not been there long when they wheeled in a young man in his thirties accompanied by his beautiful wife and their lovely four-year-old daughter. The debilitation of his once handsome body was all but complete. He could no longer speak, but with the limited motion he still had in his hand, he typed messages to his family on a keyboard connected to his motorized chair. He had lost the ability to hold up his head, so a metal vice surrounding his head held it in place. His deep-set eyes appeared to be the only part of his body that functioned properly, and they constantly followed the movements of his daughter. His wife acted cheerful and smiled at those about her, but the sadness in her eyes overshadowed all other messages she tried to send. The little girl stayed close by her father's side and talked to him as though at any moment his ability to speak miraculously would return. Eventually they came for her father, wheeled him into the examination room and closed the door. The moment they closed the door between her and her father, the little girl began to cry. She cried softly at first and then her sobs could be heard throughout the lobby as she beat on the door. Mercifully for her, someone opened the door and she was permitted to rejoin her father. I will forever be haunted by that moment, for I know that soon a door will be shut between the little girl and her father that no one can open.

Today I sent the following letter to a hundred people. ALS may never be affected by it, but at least I threw a punch. Just maybe in the future it will help keep another little girl's door from being shut.

A Letter to Friends:

I am writing you on a matter of great importance to Veleda and me. As some of you know, I was told about a year ago that I have ALS, or Lou Gehrig's disease. There is currently no effective treatment for this fatal disease which affects about 100,000 Americans. No one knew what caused ALS when it killed the "Pride of the Yankees" in 1941, and its cause remains a mystery today. Given the circumstances, we are doing well and plan to live each day to the fullest.

The purpose of this letter is to ask you to consider becoming involved in a quest for hope. Millions of Americans each year die or live in debilitated states because of ALS, Parkinson's disease, multiple sclerosis, diabetes, lymphoma, and spinal cord injuries. These illnesses have two common traits: (1) they have the ability to destroy lives, thereby demoralizing families, and (2) they may be cured through advances in stem cell research. Given the time constraints, stem cell research will likely not save me or shield my family from the devastating effects of ALS, but there is hope...real hope now for the future that we have never had before.

As you know, today stem cell research is linked to scientific, religious, and political agendas. I value your friendship too much to try to badger you into thinking as I do on this matter, but I will prevail on our friendship to ask you to think about the issues associated with research that is critically important to millions of Americans.

Long ago Plato cautioned us that great civilizations never emerged from the power of opinion but through a passionate search for knowledge. Quite simply, when we cling to our comfort zones, when we rely on what others tell us without questioning, we are probably working from opinions. When we question beliefs, when we analyze for ourselves, when we search for meaning, we have some hope of reaching the knowledge level. Whether you choose to oppose or support the development of stem cell research, I hope you do so from a basis of knowledge. If you want to study this issue, I urge you to examine the abundant online data and to consider the following:

- *Stem cell research does not mean a fetus is destroyed. Research occurs at the cellular level.*
- *Because of current government regulations, tissue that could be used in stem cell research is thrown away daily.*
- *No significant amount of stem cell research can occur without government subsidies.*

My neurologist is a wonderful Christian who supports stem cell research. She is very competent and makes every effort to stay abreast of developments in the field. Even with all her skills, though, she can only treat the symptoms of her patients, for no cure for ALS exists. Perhaps stem cell research hold the key to finding that cure.

If you are interested in becoming involved, you may do so by contacting your senators and your representatives in Washington. Attached you will find information from Texans for Advanced Medical Research (TAMR), which summarizes pending stem cell legislation in Austin and the names and addresses of Texas leaders.

Jim Boyd

July 8, 2005

Shortly after sunset today, I was driving through the pasture in the ATV. In the light of my headlights, I noticed a great horned owl on the ground beside the trail. At first he paid me no mind, but as I got closer his giant wings gracefully lifted him into the air. As he became airborne, a snake frantically tried to free himself from the death grip of the owl's talons. The owl and the snake disappeared into the night sky.

The incident reminded me of the legend surrounding the founding of Mexico City. According to the legend, the god of the Aztecs commanded the people to build a holy city at the site where they would find an eagle grasping a serpent. One day in the highlands of Central Mexico, villagers came upon an eagle lifting a snake into the heavens. On this spot they built Tenochtitlán, "the holy place," which eventually became Mexico City.

I do not think God commanded the owl to ensnare the snake, but I do know that God lives along the pasture road. I feel his presence every morning when I walk in the rising sun. I see his work in the craggy landscape where living things tenaciously cling to life. I hear God speak when nature's chorus begins with the breaking of the new day. I don't know that I have ever been in a place where God speaks to me more clearly.

AUGUST 5, 2005

Between my junior and senior years in high school I landed a job with the U.S. Forest Service in Montana. Since that job wouldn't begin until the middle of June, I worked for a few weeks at a Texaco service station. One block away, my friend David Killen worked in his father's service station, which sold gas at a discounted rate. If I remember correctly, their price was about twenty-two cents per gallon, or several cents below other stations in town. I had not worked at the station for very long when a man from the corporate offices arrived. He began to talk with the station owner about what all the "cheap gas" was doing to their profit margins. I was in and out of the station during this conversation, but I heard enough to understand that something needed to be done with this kind of competition.

Before they could take action, they needed proof to show how cheaply gas was being sold at Killen's station. That is where I came into the picture; the "company man" walked up to me and gave me two dollars. He told me to drive my car over to Killen's discount station, purchase two dollars' worth of gasoline and to ask for a cash receipt. In those days in Round Rock,

Texas, no one ever asked for a cash receipt for anything. I could just imagine what my friend David would think as he watched me drive one block from my station to his to buy two dollars' worth of gas and then demand a cash receipt. He would know something was up, and I did not want to be a part of the scheme. I told my boss I would not do what he wanted me to do. At this point the "company man" became very indignant and said, "Never mind, I'll do it myself." While he was gone my boss, who was disgusted with the way I had acted, proceeded to tell me what a dumb thing I had done. I was chastised for being rude, and then as if in some way the "company man" needed to be defended, he said, "That's a very important person, and he is a lot bigger man than you'll ever be."

I have thought a great deal about that remark over the years. My boss might not have said what he did had he not been angry, but in reality I think he was echoing the sentiments of a lot of people in our community. People from working-class families were not expected to amount to much. In the eyes of my old boss, I probably never did measure up to the "company man." I don't know that I could have if I had tried. What I do know is that looking back over my years as an educator, I feel a lot better about my journey than I would have had I spent my time trying to manipulate gas prices.

September 27, 2005

Each morning on the pasture road I see evidence of those who passed this way in the night. In the loose sand of the pathway, the tracks of raccoons tell of their nightly patrols looking for meals and mischief. The hoof marks of deer are always there and sometimes I can see they were trailed by coyotes or a bobcat. In warm weather, lazy S's in the road are reminders to beware; this is rattlesnake country. If you look closely enough, you can see that even the tiniest of trackers like centipedes and dung beetles leave their marks on the road. As the day plays itself out, wind, traffic, and sometimes rain will erase from history all evidence of the previous night.

I once knew a girl in high school; let's say her name was…Jane. Because of her commitment to the straight and narrow, she was referred to by some people as "no tracks in the snow" Jane. I do not know if she ever strayed from her declared course. At least she never did when she was with me. But she did leave tracks. We all leave tracks.

The problem with human tracks is that unlike those in the road, they are often permanent. Knowingly or unknowingly, we leave our markers for future generations. Long ago Greeks saw history as a stage occupied by humans who were either plunderers or builders. Plunderers have no regard for those who follow and live for the moment. America's most listened-to radio broadcaster, talking about energy consumption recently, asked the question, "Why should we inconvenience ourselves? We deserve what we have." No doubt Americans are industrious people, and we can be proud of the standard of living we have created; it is unparalleled in history. But who is going to repay the enormous national debt we're building? Who is going to repair the ozone layer we're destroying? Where will we get clean water when the aquifers are depleted? We think we own this land, but in truth the land owns us, all of us, and as we have learned from the Native Americans, the land always claims its rent. A plundering society ignores its inheritance as it defers sacrifice to its children.

It might be said that as individuals we leave our tracks on and within other people. We leave our tracks on others around us when we ignore their subtle pleas for some affirmation of worth in their lives. We leave our tracks on others when we use them as stepping-stones along our path to glory.

Most of the college professors I worked with over the years were conscientious professionals dedicated to their students. In the main, I was honored just to be listed among their ranks. The few exceptions I knew still stand out vividly in my mind. These individuals used, and sometimes abused, their students on a self-centered path to professional recognition. In the name of academic freedom and with the protection of tenure, some of them tortured their students with twenty-year-old lectures unworthy at the time of origin and irrelevant to the present. Some ignored students' needs and spent most of their time on lucrative research projects or consulting. In these unfortunate cases, the tracks they left on their students were markers of their disregard for people who deserved better.

We also leave our tracks within others when we touch their hearts. One way we touch hearts is when we seek to discover the good in other people. When we have touched the hearts of other people, theirs are the lights that we let shine. If a person is better off for having had the opportunity to know us, the chances are we left our tracks in the right place. Once I heard someone say that the real mark of a man is how he treats those who can't do anything for him. I have always thought this to be the real definition of *class* and ultimately a marker for tracks left in the right place.

Like all people I know, I have left tracks on both sides of the road. As I think back on a long journey, I have learned that we walk in a "magnetic field." There are forces out there, both left and right, that constantly seek to pull us from our center. Our center is the inner core within each of us that assumes command in times of crisis and when values are at stake. A person who never seeks to define his or her center will succumb to the magnetic field. We find the center only when we seek to look beyond ourselves. The truly happy people I have known are those who knew their center before they began their journey.

SEPTEMBER 28, 2005

Thirty years ago on a hot August day Veleda's uncle, Walter Brandenberger, came to the ranch. At that time he was in his late eighties, but like most members of his family, he was still spry, agile, and full of life despite advancing age. Uncle Walter was familiar with the ranch, for as a youth he had ridden every inch of it while managing Grandfather Brandenberger's cattle. Children were always intrigued by the missing finger on his right hand, which made its exit when it became entangled in the reins of a runaway horse. He never talked much about his experience as a soldier in World War I, although I tried numerous times to get him to talk about what he had seen on the Western Front.

The primary topic of conversation that day was the summer drought that had parched the earth and dried up all but a few watering holes. When we told him that Panther Creek, the primary source for water on the ranch, had been reduced to a single watering place at the spring near the northern border of the pasture, he began to talk about the drought of 1919 that was so devastating to ranchers. He talked about how our spring had held out throughout that long dry spell, when almost all other sources of water had disappeared.

He sparked everyone's attention when he said, "We had to dig for water that summer in 1919." "But where?" we asked. "Well, I'll have to show you," he said. In short order, with pick and shovel in hand, we drove to the place we call the Kettle, near the old rock fence. Here Uncle Walter walked into the middle of the creek bed and began to poke around in the gravel. In a few moments he located a limestone ledge that traversed the creek bed. In the crevice next to the ledge he began to shovel away at the gravel. In no more than a few minutes, water began to bubble up from where he was digging. Not long thereafter we had a trough about 10 feet long, one foot wide, and one foot deep filled with water. That much water would not sustain the herd and wildlife needs, but it would help. Seeing it also lifted our spirits.

With another drought now robbing us of precious water in the creek, last week my son Jeff and I went to the same place and opened the crevice again. In short order there was water where only the crusty scale of a creek bed had existed before. This treasure would have been lost forever had Uncle Walter not come to the ranch on that hot August day.

The information Uncle Walter shared with us is what I call "generational learning." I believe that generational learning is the most significant of all knowledge a person can acquire. The really important things to know about in life, such as faith in God, love of family, the ethic of work, family culture, and traditions, are most commonly transmitted through generational learning.

One vivid example of what I am talking about is the transmission of generational knowledge among the Moken people in Southeast Asia. Better known as the Sea Gypsies, these people spend all of their lives living on boats or in stilt houses extending out into the sea. Most have no formal education and live their lives depending on generational knowledge to provide for their tribes. This knowledge was the primary reason no one in the tribe was lost when the tsunami of 2005 devastated the area where they lived. Shortly before the tidal wave came ashore, one of the village elders noticed a rapid receding of the shoreline. He also noted that all sounds of wildlife in the area had abated. In his lifetime he had never witnessed a tsunami, but he recalled stories told to him by his forefathers that these were signs of an approaching tidal wave. He immediately began sounding the alarm among those about him. At first everyone thought he was crazy, and some accused him of being drunk, but they obeyed his command to go farther inland. Shortly thereafter, the tidal wave hit, destroying everything along the shore. At sea, other Mokens who had learned the signs from their ancestors quickly sailed into deeper water where they were safe from the effects of the tidal wave building beneath them.[12]

It is also interesting to note that the Moken language does not include the words *worry, when,* or *want.*[13] I can only surmise that their culture evolved from previous generations that deemed these words to have no value. We see the Mokens as primitive people, but how superior is our culture where life is so subservient to those three words?

Today we are losing access to, and wisdom from, generational learning. Families have become so fragmented that often the base for generational learning no longer exists. The link between parent and child may be there, but too often there is no bridge to the collective wisdom of the past.

We are also producing a new generation of children whose addiction to electronic media is so strong that there is little room in their environment for anything but entertainment. I see children in malls and I wonder if iPods are not a new appendage growing from their ears. The computers in their rooms designed to link them with the World Wide Web are, in reality, driving them farther and farther into small cells that isolate them from the world. Ultimately, entertainment opiates have the power to create microworlds in which the need for social interaction and relationship building are minuscule. In that environment, generational learning dies a quick death.

SEPTEMBER 29, 2005

We all live with the objective of being happy. Our lives are all different and yet the same.—Anne Frank[14]

During the time when I was a college president, our institution was offered an opportunity to be the American host for the International Anne Frank Exhibit. The exhibit was a collection of photographs and memorabilia on loan from a museum in Amsterdam. I could hardly contain my excitement when I learned we might have an opportunity to be a part of telling the story of the young Jewish girl who had captured the imagination of the world. The diary she left behind when taken to a Nazi concentration camp is a compelling account of an adolescent girl's innocence, hopes, and fears. Though she, along with most members of her family, died at the hands of her Nazi captors, her legacy has inspired millions to stand in the face of tyranny. My excitement for this project heightened when I also learned Meip Geist was considering a speaking engagement on our campus during the time of the exhibit. By any measure, Meip Geist is an authentic heroine. During the Frank family's two long years of hiding, it was Meip Geist who daily risked her life to bring food to the eight people in the attic. Her story of that turbulent time is a monumental account of courage in the face of fear and extraordinary commitment to those in need.

Weatherford, Texas, always seems to rest in the shadows of Fort Worth and Dallas, so it seemed to me we had a golden opportunity to put our community and our institution in the national spotlight. Most of the people I talked with shared my enthusiasm for what this opportunity might mean. There were, however, some major contingencies associated with our hosting the event. Though we would house the collection in our library, there were complex security issues to handle. We also had to raise a substantial amount of money to underwrite the project.

During the time I was president, I enjoyed a good working relationship with community leaders. In fact, I would have to say the community treated me much better than I deserved. There was, however, one political figure in the community who did not share my sentiments for the exhibit or, for that matter, most things I wanted to do. Not long after word got out about our plans to host the exhibit, this person came to my office intent on telling me we should have nothing to do with the project. It would serve no good purpose for me to describe why this person felt we should not bring the Anne Frank exhibit to our community, but suffice it to say I was livid when the meeting was over. The lines were drawn in the sand and we both began to look for allies.

In retrospect, I should have known then that I could not muster the political support essential for bringing the exhibit to our campus. My anger prevailed, however, and I charged on into a fight and, when the dust settled, I was left scarred and defeated. A number of people were enthused about the project and we might have gotten by had I been able to raise the money necessary to underwrite the project, but that didn't work out.

As I was licking my wounds, a person who was a strong supporter of the Anne Frank exhibit came to my office. To my amazement, she told me that Meip Geist had heard about our failed efforts, and she was sympathetic to our cause and willing to include our institution on an upcoming speaking tour of the United States. I could not contain my excitement. By any measure Meip Geist was a major player on the world's stage, and she was coming to speak to our students.

I shall never forget the night she came to campus. It was a Friday night, which meant party night for most college students, so we were worried about the number of people who would choose to come to the event. We were pleased that a large number of community members began to promote the event. An hour before the program was scheduled to start, people began to pour into the gymnasium, which was eventually filled to capacity.

Veleda and I had the opportunity to visit with Meip before the event and found her to be utterly charming. In her eighty-eighth year she still radiated enthusiasm, energy, and extraordinary depth of thought. Her limited English and Veleda's limited

German created an avenue for conversation that I shall never forget. Of all of the people I have ever met, Meip Geist had the strongest sense of presence. I felt honored to be in her company and, as I would learn later in the evening, would be deeply touched by her words.

Her presentation that night was basically a firsthand account of Anne Frank's story, which had touched the hearts of millions of people through Anne's posthumously published diary. Meip talked of Nazi terror, betrayal, and of a compelling love for the family of Anne Frank. I doubt anyone in the audience left unmoved by her words.

She concluded her remarks by telling of what hate and an unforgiving nature can do to the human heart. She related a postwar story about how the loss of her Jewish friends had caused her to hate all Germans. In particular she talked about her own outburst against a German family who had come to see the now world-famous hiding place, after the war ended. At that point, Otto Frank, the sole survivor from the hiding place, reprimanded her for her tirade and said, "Do you not know that this German family was also placed in a Nazi concentration camp?" In effect, he was saying to her, "When you make generalizations about individuals you do not know, you too can become a racist." Or in other words, "We can often become that which we despise if we allow ourselves to be ruled by hate and anger." Her remarks were followed by a sustained ovation that lasted several minutes.

Later that night I did not sleep well, for I could not keep from reflecting on what Meip had said during her moving presentation. I think what impressed me the most about her was not her heroism, but what she had become from the experience. Despite the enormous losses she knew in her years of terror at the hands of the Nazis, she was not a bitter person. She understood how enormously important it was to move forward from a troubled past without letting it destroy your inner being. In that moment I also came to realize that compared to Meip Geist, some of the things I had been letting bother me were incredibly insignificant. In particular, I was disappointed in myself for the grudge I still carried over the loss of the Anne Frank Exhibit. In reality the only person really being affected by it was Jim Boyd. I would not say Meip Geist changed my unforgiving nature, but she helped me gain a perspective that began my recovery from my disappointment over losing the exhibit.

OCTOBER 10, 2005

Last week the Pentagon announced that two thousand Americans have now died in the Iraq war. Like all Americans, I was deeply grieved by the announcement. Hours before the milestone was made public, President George W. Bush said that war will require more sacrifice, time, and resolve.

My question is "Whose sacrifice are we talking about?" No doubt the armed forces and their families are making enormous sacrifices for their fellow citizens. Our troops have demonstrated, time after time, that they are willing to go anywhere at any time to confront any threat to our flag. We owe them all of the respect we can muster from the depths of our soul, and in the end, that still will not be enough.

Our people are getting killed every day, yet I feel no participation in this war. Unless they have family involved, most Americans feel little connection to this war. By and large we are not even inconvenienced by this conflict. When sacrifices are called for, they should be made by all of us—not just a few. If the call for "more sacrifice, more time, and more resolve" is something other than political rhetoric, then we should take steps to see that all Americans are affected. At a minimum, we should begin by paying the enormous war debt destined to be passed on to our grandchildren. Perhaps we should reconsider the draft. I would feel much better about things if we would ration gasoline. There is enough time in the lives of all of us to do public service, if not directly for our troops, then for their often-neglected families.

This is *America's* war. It could have been more than that, but we squandered the "9/11 goodwill" of the world through our arrogance and shortsighted leadership. Any student of history should have known an attack on Saddam Hussein, as vile as he is, would ignite religious furor throughout the Muslim world. Our problem is we work from old models. Leadership entails more than stimulus-response thinking, for ultimately we have to be concerned about long-term consequences. This is particularly true when you're dealing with an insurgency that will force you to fight an urban war in the midst of civilians. Any long-term solution to the problems in the Middle East will begin with an understanding of the culture that has prevailed there for over a thousand years.

In the name of Christianity, the English King Richard the Lionhearted led his Crusaders into the Holy Land in 1191.[15] He slashed and burned his way through the region, terrorizing the population and sacking the cities. At one point he marched twenty-seven hundred Muslim prisoners out onto the desert and executed them in a public spectacle. The Muslim leader Saladin, fearing he could not stop the Crusaders, retreated into Jerusalem where he prepared to martyr his people in defense of the holy city. Twice Richard the Lionhearted led his army to the gates of Jerusalem, only to withdraw each time without battle. Why would he retreat with the prize so close at hand? He knew quick military victories would not bring an end to hostilities in a region where warfare against Western influence has fused cultural, religious, and national identities. He realized, as we should have realized, that ultimately we would have to occupy whatever territories we conquered. No army, regardless of its strength, can occupy hostile territory thousands of miles from its supply base and not encounter monumental resistance. The British learned this in 1776; Nazi Germany and Napoleon both learned this in the Russian winters outside of Moscow; and we learned it in Vietnam.

I think that ultimately, with the right diplomacy, we could have enlisted the support of other Arab and several European countries in our efforts to deal with Iraq. In many ways, Saddam Hussein was more a threat to the Middle East than he was to us. It seems that no thought was given to the fact that by deposing Saddam Hussein ourselves we have in effect eliminated Iran's time-honored enemy, thereby freeing that rogue nation to turn all its venom on us. As it is, we have now created a struggle between East and West. With a clear perspective on history and better leadership, we could have established a collaborative effort among responsible nations to get rid of a two-bit dictator. I suspect sometime before the next presidential election

Washington will announce some kind of victory and bring most all of our troops home. We will leave behind at least 2,000 of our brave soldiers as well as 30,000 dead Iraqi soldiers and 600,000 civilians. The United States is now a lightning rod for Muslim hatred around the world, and future generations will pay the price for what we have done. It could have been different.

DECEMBER 12, 2005

Sometimes dreams do come true and prayers are answered. Chad and Amy, and grandsons Christian and Thomas, are moving back to Texas from Oregon. They will live here on the ranch in the bunkhouse and Chad will work as a biologist for the Texas Parks and Wildlife Department. We will share the evening meal together like the Waltons, and the two boys will now have the run of the ranch. There will be continuation here. We rejoice and thank God for our good fortune.

DECEMBER 15, 2005

Long ago I spent a very rewarding year teaching at the Randolph Air Force Base high school. The students there had traveled all over the world and had seen many of the places I talked about in our history and government classes. All of the students were sons and daughters of Air Force personnel and were therefore expected to toe the line where regulations were concerned. Like all Texas schools, RHS was football-crazy. A large portion of the student body, one way or another, was active on Friday football nights.

I shall never forget one of my Randolph students. His name was Morrison Rigdon Woods, and he didn't fit the mold. He was smaller than most of the boys in his class. He made excellent grades, though I suspect he seldom studied. The length of his fiery red hair pressed the rigid school dress code a bit. Behind the steel-rimmed glasses he wore were mischievous eyes. Any person who looked into those eyes knew something was always working behind the scenes. Though he could have cared less about the rah-rah high school atmosphere, he was well liked by the other students.

Toward the end of the school year, Morrison decided to begin publishing an underground school newspaper. With due respect to his journalistic abilities, I do not recall anything about his story line, other than it was not supportive of the status quo. Needless to say, school authorities made sure that Morrison had a short, yet rather glorious, career as a newspaper publisher.

Thirty years later, my wife and I had a very pleasant dinner with Morrison and his lovely wife. In the intervening years, middle age had settled over both him and me, but the gleam in his eye was still there. Over the years I had often thought about Morrison. In particular, I was curious as to what his father, an Air Force master sergeant, thought about his earlier venture into journalism. During the course of the evening, my curiosity gave way to an inquiry. I do not remember exactly how Morrison responded, but it went something like this: "When we talked about what had happened with the paper, my father said he did not agree with what I was writing, but that he had fought in two wars to ensure my right to say what I wanted to say." He left the matter at that.

Have we as a nation lost Sergeant Woods's wisdom? I would like to think it is still out there, but as I watch the evening news or listen to AM radio, I wonder. Our nation, above all others, has taught the world about tolerance. Yet today, saying what a person believes can easily get one branded as unpatriotic, non-Christian, too conservative, or too liberal. To make matters worse, the political-correctness watchdogs are always there ready, at the least provocation, to derail a career. Honest debate among politicians is largely a thing of the past, for most of them have succumbed to "the politics of personal destruction." Or in other words, if you can link your opponent with the bad guys, you don't have to stand for much to win.

Presidents Lincoln, Eisenhower, and Carter, and Senators Glenn, Murtha, and Goldwater were among those who risked their lives on the battlefield and their political fortunes in Washington to fight intolerance. In their lives, we can find lessons for a nation.

DECEMBER 17, 2005

It seems as though I was never strong. I see people around me casually lift things that I can no longer budge. For me, the force of gravity has increased tenfold. My left arm hangs limply at my side now as though it were a broken wing. My right arm is in a tenacious fight. He knows what is at stake if he loses, and because he doesn't want to let me down, he tries desperately to function. With each day, though, he is less than what he had been. It has been so long now. Sometimes it seems that this is the way my arms have always been.

My legs remain strong, and they carry me to places on the ranch. Along the way I see cedar trees cut to the ground, fence posts protruding from holes punched through limestone ledges, native grasses growing where wild persimmon once prevailed. No, things *were* different once. In a way I have lived two lifetimes: one long life that was too short, and another brief life that has been too long.

JANUARY 2, 2006

In a recent television program, journalist Barbara Walters revealed the names on her list of "The 10 Most Fascinating People for the Year 2005." Her selections included Secretary of State Condoleezza Rice and cyclist Lance Armstrong, but it was overwhelmingly dominated by Hollywood personalities and London royalty. For the most part, Ms. Walters discovered that the most fascinating people in the world are those who regularly appear in the tabloids. In her opinion, Camilla Parker Bowles was the most fascinating person in the world for 2005. Given her contributions to humanity, I am sure Madame Bowles's selection came as quite a revelation to those in the United Kingdom.

This is indeed a fascinating list, for I am awed by some of the questions it raises. For instance, what sorting process did Ms. Walters use to eliminate the approximately one billion people who live in China? Given the odds, I would have thought at least one person on this planet from outside the United States or England would have qualified.

I am greatly amazed that among those brave souls in Iraq and Afghanistan who stand in harm's way every moment of the day defending our country, she found no one fascinating enough for her list. She found no candidate among the millions of teachers, some of whom daily work in war zones of their own, worthy of consideration. No mention was made of the relief workers who worked night and day in the wake of Hurricane Katrina or those who give freely of their time to fight disease and starvation in the Sudan. Among the winners of this year's Nobel Prize, who will shape the future of our world, she found no one of great fascination.

What is to be said for Ms. Walter's selections? My sense is that the prism through which she views the world allows her to see nothing but her own kind. I don't think the woman gets around much.

January 5, 2006

A friend of mine once told me an interesting story about his father's funeral. His father was a respected citizen and a prominent businessman in their community, so a large number of people attended the funeral. After the services, several individuals came to the family to tell them of their respect for his dad. One of those who came was an elderly Hispanic man who had worked several years for my friend's dad. My friend could not speak much Spanish, and the elderly man could speak very little English. Though the words did not flow clearly, it was obvious from the man's gestures and the mist in his eyes that he was trying to tell my friend of his deep affection for his father. Finally, the old gentleman, mustering the few English words he knew, said, "Your daddy, he do what he say." After that, nothing else needed to be said, for one of the highest compliments in both cultures had been given. Even when he told me this story some years later, my friend was still deeply moved by the message.

I suspect the message was more than "your daddy kept his word." The message was really about the respect given to people who honor their word and live what they say. In a similar vein, the cattlemen of South Texas often described an honorable man by saying that "He covered the ground he stood on." We trust these people. In a world where trust for all institutions has steadily declined since the 1960s, perhaps there is a lesson here.

Chapter 3
The Gift of Trust

The more credible you are, the more confidence people place in you, thereby allowing you the privilege of influencing their lives.—John Maxwell[1]

Leaders improve organizations primarily through relationships. After food, water, and shelter, the quality of our relationships most often determines our quality of life.[2] Trust is the bond that holds enduring relationships together. It is a very fragile commodity—difficult to attain, yet easy to lose. Trust is also something others unequivocally expect to have in leaders, and from the viewpoint of followers, either it is there or it is not there. No CEO ever got a job by looking the board squarely in the eye and saying, "You can trust me...most of the time."

The time has long since passed when a person assuming a leadership position would automatically inherit a large measure of trust. Trust, if it develops, will do so only over time, and then it will come as a gift, not as a prize.

An infinite variety of variables affect how trust, or the lack of it, comes to exist in any organization. Trust is not the product of management strategies, nor is it greatly influenced by rank within the organization. It is much more about what a person is than what he or she does. Trusted leaders are seldom ostentatious, flamboyant, or egotistical, champing at the bit to make some new and dramatic decision.[3] Unpredictable leaders often create schizophrenic organizations.

Earning the Trust of Others

In *The Servant as Leader*, Robert Greenleaf wrote that a leader's ability to nurture trust comes from a confidence others have in his or her values, judgment, and a "sustaining spirit." It is the presence of, and the predictability of, these three elements of character that sustain a trusting environment.[4]

Values

Trusted leaders do not wait for their defining moments to identify values that mark their lives. They are the same people, regardless of where they are, who they are with, or what pressures come to play in their lives.[5] They are known for their integrity, honesty, and compassion. Trusted leaders seek to discover and recognize the contributions of others; they make choices that will benefit the organization when another choice would have benefited the leader. Mahatma Gandhi understood what it meant to lead a value-laden life. He was small in stature and led no army, but the values he lived by inspired a nation to claim its freedom.

Judgment

A leader can be well meaning and have noble values and still not be trusted by followers. We trust leaders who make good decisions, on their feet, at the scene of the battle. Trusted leaders never shy away from making difficult decisions that may displease the perpetual "failure forecasters" within organizations. Their focus is on the greater good of the organization, not on popularity. Many of Lincoln's decisions were opposed on both sides of the Mason-Dixon Line. Lincoln, however, thought on a higher plane than most people. In the end, his superior judgment and his courage to make difficult decisions saved the Union.[6]

Sustaining Spirit

Trusted leaders are known by their unrelenting personal will. Once the pathway has been identified for the organization, the company, or the family, the leader will not be deterred. Trusted leaders reject victim mentalities and spend their energies thinking in terms of possibilities. They also set high standards of performance for each person in the organization and hold them accountable. Some historians maintain that the greatest leadership feat of the past century was accomplished by the Antarctic explorer Sir Ernest Shackleton. When his ship sank in the Antarctic Ocean not far from the South Pole, he matter-of-factly told his men that if they would trust him, he would get them home. He spent the next year traveling across the pack ice and in rough seas to eventually lead his twenty-eight men to safety. For 522 days his ship had been out of port, and the men had long since been given up for lost and presumed dead. His men later recalled that Shackleton was the embodiment of confidence and a sustaining spirit.[7]

As writer John Maxwell reminds us, "The more credible you are, the more confidence people place in you, thereby allowing you the privilege of influencing their lives."[8] Whether the leader is called superintendent, general, CEO, or parent, in the end others will decide if they are worthy of trust.

Losing the Trust of Others

In all human interactions, what people give, they can also take away. This is particularly true with issues of trust. The matter is further complicated by the fact that on any given day, good people, well deserving of our trust, can be blindsided by an issue that puts their integrity into question. In a society quick to judge leaders in the public eye, perceptions often become realities, and when this happens there is usually a price to be paid.

We can't do much about people who are untrustworthy, but hopefully the system will eventually take care of them. There are things we can do, though, to help ensure others do not consign us to the ranks of the untrustworthy. Three suggestions follow.

Mirrors and Windows

We tend to distrust people who look in the mirror when credit is due and through the window when blame is to be assessed. In highly effective organizations, leaders are known for reflecting credit from themselves to others.[9] In their daily lives they are on a perpetual search to discover the good things others are doing for the organization, and they make every effort to provide them recognition. When things are not going well, trusted leaders first look in the mirror. If they perpetually look for scapegoats through the window, trust within the organization is at risk.[10]

Not long after I became president of Weatherford College, I was told we had a problem in one of our programs. No fraud was involved and there had been no malicious intent on the part of the staff, but the problem was serious enough that I asked my board chairman to come to my office for a briefing on the situation. We were sitting on the sofa in my office when I began to explain the situation to him. I told him briefly about the problem and was in the process of saying something like, "I am sure I could have headed this off had I been here long enough to understand how the system works." I never finished this sentence, as the board chairman abruptly raised his hand and pointed to the president's desk across the room. "You see that desk over there?" he asked. I nodded my head. "The person responsible for this problem sits in that chair," he said quite sternly. That was not exactly the message I wanted to hear from my boss, but it was one of the most important lessons of leadership I was ever taught. In the years thereafter, whatever problems arose at the college, I could never separate myself from the advice I was given that day. I suspect a few times I even took bullets that rightfully belonged to someone else, but I felt good about the view through the window.

Hidden Agendas

We resent hidden agendas, whether they appear in casual relationships or organizational activity.[11] Trusted leaders do not work from hidden agendas, but they can still be hurt when perceptions of them develop. While no one may say it, when we appoint a committee filled with people who share our opinions, perceptions of hidden agendas develop. Similar perceptions thrive in environments when the leader placates subordinates by asking for input on decisions everyone knows have already been made. One way to help avoid perceptions of hidden agendas is to find someone in the organization who has the courage to "speak truth to power."[12] This type of individual is incredibly valuable to leadership, and every effort should be made to gain that person's confidence. Ask this person what he or she thinks about the way a proposed initiative will unfold. You will likely get good advice.

Creating False Hopes

Do not tell subordinates or your children they have the power to do something if you really don't mean it.[13] Despite its noble purpose, the shared-governance movement continues to create trust issues for leaders. Unless we identify in advance the rules and relationships for all parties in the empowerment process, there are enormous possibilities for distrust developing. I still bear scars from my failures to establish clear parameters associated with employee-empowerment initiatives. The first order of business should be to identify the rules to be followed when the power has been granted, and under what circumstances it can be taken back. Second, if new roles are assigned, what will be the new responsibility and accountability measures associated with empowerment? These principles apply to the granting of power to leadership teams, sovereign states, or a teenage son about to use the family car for the first time.

Trust is much easier lost than gained, and once it is lost, it is difficult—if not impossible—to get it back. Leaders who build trusting organizations do so by accepting the fact that *trust is a gift on loan*, a loan that may be called in at any moment. They also know that trust does not evolve from random acts, but through choices leaders make and values they exhibit. Accordingly, each day servant leaders live in such a way that they affirm for others their worthiness of trust.[14]

JANUARY 6, 2006

We have had less than two inches of rain in the last six months. Nothing in the pasture is green, and almost all of the watering places in the creek are dry. Texas is a droughty state, and historically, one in three years produces less-than-desirable rainfall, but I remember nothing comparable to this. Even in the dramatic droughts of the 1950s, the scant rainfall was more evenly distributed. If we had not taken good care of our pasture, there would be nothing for the cattle to eat except prickly pear. Though rainfall totals have sometimes been above average, we have had only one good year in seven. Too often our rain has come in torrents when we didn't need it, and long dry spells during growing season have stressed the range, water wells, livestock, and all manner of wildlife. I worry about the people whose wells are going dry, for many of them will have to sell their cattle.

Many seem to see no association between the "hundred-year floods," which now regularly occur, and the fact that the aquifer recharge zones are covered with too little grass and too much concrete to sustain nature's way. Hydrologists know, ranchers know, people with common sense know that if we wanted to cooperate with nature, we could alter this cycle. But doing so would require major shifts in thinking about the way we manage land and control development. I fear there are too many people with swimming pools and too few people with water troughs to make a difference.

JANUARY 8, 2006

Some things are bad even when they are not against the law.
—William F. Buckley[15]

House Majority Leader Tom DeLay, amid allegations of unethical behavior and corruption, has announced he will relinquish his leadership post in the House of Representatives. I am no authority on Tom DeLay because all I know about him comes from the press, which is to say I don't know much. If he is guilty of the corrupt use of his enormous powers, there should be consequences. That is someone else's call, not mine.

What bothers me the most about the situation is not what he allegedly did illegally; it is what he and others like him readily admit they have done legally for years. What we have here is an indictment of the corporate state in which we now live.

Influence in Washington is for sale, lobbyists are placing orders, and the American people are paying the bill. Because most Americans cannot afford a multimillion-dollar campaign, the enormous sums of money collected at fundraisers return incumbents to office each election. To put this in perspective, in the last election nine out of ten congressional incumbents were re-elected.[16] That percentage is roughly equivalent to the rate of reelection for Communist Party members in the former Soviet Union. During the recent elections in the Middle East, one reporter overheard prospective voters discussing the topic of "one man, one vote." Thinking he was observing democracy in action, he followed the conversation closely, only to learn that what "one man, one vote" really meant to them was "if you vote Islamic fundamentalists into office one time, you'll never get them out of office." My point here is not to equate American politicians to Communists or Islamic fundamentalists, but I am questioning a system that perpetually returns the same people to office each year.

Today, no corporation in this country could survive using the congressional model. Dynamic organizations stay competitive through the infusion of new talent and creativity, and the upward mobility of competent leaders. Given the leadership stagnation caused by the seniority system, special-interest power brokers, and partisan politics, Congress and most state governments wouldn't last six months as private entities in the competition-driven world economy. To put it another way, a recent Gallup poll indicated that less than one-third of Americans now approve of the way Congress handles the nation's business.[17] If the U.S. Congress were a commercial airline, how many Americans would risk their lives by flying with them?

Anticipating a developing scandal, both parties are now scurrying to become the party of reform. Before the next election takes place, there will be legislation touted as limiting lobbyists' access to elected officials. While the impression will be conveyed that Congress is giving up its cozy relationship with lobbyists, the truth is, it doesn't mean much when a centipede gives up an arm and a leg. This is not a self-correcting problem. You cannot depend on those drinking from the trough to cut off the faucet.

Real reform, if it ever occurs, will evolve from voters rebelling against professional politicians and those who put them in power. A good start would be to limit terms of office to no more than two four-year terms. The absurd pensions and benefits that those in Congress hide for themselves in appropriation bills should be made to conform to the levels received by Social Security and/or state employee pension recipients. Throw in, for good measure, dramatic restrictions on contributions from outside congressional districts. A local election should be just that, not some referendum on what Hollywood stars think or megacorporations want.

I have never accepted the notion of collective guilt that some groups today want to impose on others. I have no more sense of guilt for what my great-great-grandfather might have done than my great-great-grandchildren should feel for any of my own shortcomings. God gave us free will and he will hold us, not others, accountable for what we do.

While I cannot accept the idea of collective guilt, I do believe in collective ignorance. This phenomenon may occur in a number of ways, but it inevitably emerges when those in a democracy excuse greed, corruption, and exploitation in their leaders. A collective wisdom would tell us that the mistakes made in ancient Athens or Rome and by the British Empire do not have to be played out in our own history. We can never repay those who gave us this republic, for they now rest in eternity, but we can honor their memory by protecting the future.

JANUARY 10, 2006

On the far side of Panther Creek there is a place we call Horace's Bluff. It's really not much of a bluff, for it rises no more than fifteen or twenty feet above the creek bed. Its distinction comes from the red sand, which contrasts with the clusters of live-oak trees around it, and a story from one hot August day. The incident involves Veleda's cousin Horace Brandenberger, one of the most memorable characters I have known.

Horace and I were friends for more than forty-five years, and during that time I came to appreciate him for a number of reasons, not the least of which was the fact that he had the courage to be himself. I don't think anyone who knew him would say that he spent a lot of time listening to the standard drummer's cadence.

Horace's German immigrant ancestors settled on the banks of Beaver Creek in Mason County, Texas, in the 1850s. As with his father and grandfather before him, he learned German before he could speak English. His forefathers were conservative, God-fearing ranchers who worked hard, saved their money, and prospered. I met him when he was in his mid-forties, and I was immediately struck by his good looks and striking physique. Throughout most of his life, I believe his enormous strength was the primary reason he generally abandoned finesse in favor of brawn.

We were directly or indirectly involved together in the ranching business for over forty years. During that time we never had a disagreement, nor did a vile word pass between us. I say this despite the fact that he often kept records of our cattle operation by writing down numbers in the accumulated dirt on his pickup dashboard.

He also taught me more than any other person about what it means to live in harmony with the land. Historian Walter Prescott Webb, in his book *The Great Plains*, talked at length about how the land can shape the character of its caretakers.[18] I saw much of what Webb addressed played out in the way Horace lived his life. I learned from Horace that the most important thing in ranching is not the production of cattle, but the growing of grass. Even today on any of the land he owned or leased in Mason County, the wind lifts the leaves of tall grasses. Most importantly, he taught me that if you take care of the land, the land will take care of you.

Like so many people of his time, Horace grew up with an ethic for landownership that strengthened the character of ranchers, their families, and ultimately our nation. Horace was leasing the ranch from Veleda's mother and father when the terrible drought of the 1950s began. After years of prolonged drought, the ranges were barren, and many ranchers kept their cattle alive solely by burning prickly pear for them to eat. Because he saw what Horace had to endure, Veleda's father went to him one day and offered to suspend the lease payments until the drought was broken. Horace thanked him for his concern, but told him he had made a deal and intended to live up to it.

I was also struck by the harmony Horace found between the land and its creatures. We were driving cattle out of a canyon one day, I on the left side and he on the right side. It was not long before I noticed he had fallen far behind. Thinking something was wrong, I turned my horse and rode back to him. Nothing was wrong; he had just stopped to study the nest of a cactus wren nestled in a prickly pear. He appreciated the laws of nature and the harmony that exists there. I think it was that harmony that caused him to be so accepting of other people, whether they were newcomers to the family like me, hitchhikers on the side of the road, or the guys drinking morning coffee at the feed store.

Family stories abound of young Horace the daredevil. From early on he was a master horseman who could ride at breakneck speed wherever he went. Whenever he mounted a horse, it was as if the two were one being. As much as he loved horses, though, I am not sure but what he loved flying more.

He left college during World War II to join the Army Air Corps. He served with great distinction as a carrier pilot in the Pacific. He alone knew the horrors he faced there, and they affected him for the rest of his life. He did another active tour during the fifties and remained in the reserve, retiring as a lieutenant colonel.

There is little doubt that he was an excellent pilot, otherwise he would have crashed long ago when he buzzed people's houses along Beaver Creek. His neighbor Billy Bode good-naturedly tells a story of the time he had spent all morning rounding up a large herd of goats. They were about to drive the herd into the pens when all at once, out of the sky, Horace dive-bombed the goats. The animals scattered to the four winds, causing Billy to spend some time reassembling his herd.

There are some who say he once flew his plane under the narrow confines of the Llano River bridge near his home. I asked him about this rumor once, but he would not say if it was true. The fact that he did not deny the rumor made me wonder if it was true. There is no doubt in my mind he had the skill to do it if he wanted to. He also had the courage to attempt such a feat. The only thing I ever saw him afraid of was a windmill. We were working on a mill one day when he confessed to me that he was afraid of heights. I was never quite able to figure out how a man in a P-51 fighter could chase Zeros over the South Pacific, yet be afraid to climb a windmill. But that was just Horace.

While a lot of ranchers pride themselves in looking the part, Horace never gave much thought to the cowboy look. He was riding his daughter Pam's beautiful mare Cola when we met him on the road near his home one day. As was often the case, he was bare-headed, and instead of cowboy boots, he was wearing Adidas tennis shoes without socks. The leather reins on his bridle had long since passed from the scene, and on this day he guided a good horse with a nylon ski rope. The only chaps I ever saw him wear were a pair long ago discarded by his cousin Lee Roy Loeffler.

Before the advent of the sleek tandem trailers you see on the road today, many people transported livestock on the back of their pickups. The pickups in those days all had sideboards, and it was an interesting ride indeed to travel down the road with a thousand-pound cow jumping around in the bed of the pickup. Horace transported his horse in this manner. He trained his horse to jump onto the back of the pickup, which was not all that unusual for the times. What was unusual is that Horace had no endgate on his pickup. He jumped his horse into the pickup bed, and then stuck a cedar post through the sideboards and away he went. I often wondered why the horse didn't jump out of the pickup, but given how Horace drove his pickup, I suspect the horse was holding on for dear life.

One hot summer day the two of us were working cattle at the ranch. Some of the cattle did not come in, so we saddled our horses and began a search of the pasture. After an hour or so in the saddle, we and our horses were desperately thirsty. Eventually we came to the spring in the little pasture where our family has tasted cool waters for a hundred years. Horace dismounted and began to walk toward the spring. I was about to do the same when I noticed a dead deer lying at the edge of the water. I waited to see what Horace would do. He paid the deer no mind, got down on his belly, and drank his fill. When he got up I asked, "How's the water?"

"Like manna from heaven," he nonchalantly replied. At this point the unspoken question was, "Are you as wild as Horace?" I dismounted and walked over to the spring. I cannot say that the deer was in the water, but there was slime and deer hair on top of the spring water. I drank a reasonable amount of water, talked about how good it was, and got back in the saddle.

Not long after, we came upon two angora goats that had strayed into our pasture. Judging by the length of their unshorn mohair, they had probably been in there for several months. We tried to get them to move back toward the house and the pens, but the goats were not interested in what we wanted. They ran for the thick brush where they knew they could not be roped and where it was difficult to maneuver horses. Since we couldn't rope them, and I'm not saying I could have roped a goat, Horace suggested we run them to exhaustion with our horses and then catch them on foot. In the beginning his plan worked pretty well. The longer we chased the goats, the more labored their breathing and the slower their pace became. We pretty well had things going our way until the goats began to run toward the creek and the then-unnamed Horace's Bluff.

Goats are smart, and they figured they could jump from rock to rock all the way down the sheer cliff and get away from us. With Horace in the lead, we both had our horses at a dead run, trying to catch the goats before they went over the top. Eventually, given Horace's rate of speed, I became more concerned that he and his horse would go over the top of the bluff. He ran his horse all way up to the bluff's edge and jumped out of the saddle. The last thing I saw was Horace and two goats going over the edge. His riderless horse veered to the right to keep from tumbling over after them. I rode on and caught Horace's mount. When I came back, I was reluctant to look from the top of the bluff for fear of what I might find. When I did get there, I looked down to the creek bed below, and there was Horace sitting beside the two goats he had just tied up. I never asked him how he made it from the top to the bottom of the cliff without breaking his neck. You didn't ask Horace those kinds of questions. Thereafter, that place has been referred to by our family as Horace's Bluff.

Two years ago, at the age of eighty-one, Horace's health began to fail, and he decided to give up his ranching operations. There is an unwritten law in the Hill Country that you try to leave a place better than you found it. Before turning over one of his lease places to Jeff and me, Horace decided to ride the fence lines one more time to see what kind of condition they were in. His daughter Lynn and I offered to ride the fence for him, but he insisted on doing it himself. We saddled Lynn's horse and, with considerable effort, got Horace in the saddle. We were both fearful that this was a ride he did not need to take, but I have to admit when I saw him in the saddle, I saw something of the Horace I had known before. The flexed arms, the straight back, the firm chin—all those things a good horse can do to bring out dignity in a rider were all there. I was happy for him.

The ride did not end well, though. Later we found him cut and bleeding on the fence line. The horse was running wild somewhere across the fence. A treasured saddle was strewn in pieces across the pasture. With considerable effort we got him back to the pickup and made the long drive back home. I was grieved to the point of tears for him because I didn't want it to end this way. I later remarked to Lynn how badly I felt about what had happened to him on his last ride. She thought for a moment and then put matters and Horace's life in perspective by saying, "What makes you think this is his last ride?"

Where America looks for its heroes today troubles me a great deal because I think we have come to confuse celebrities with authentic heroes. Most anyone in the country can identify the leading Hollywood entertainers or television personalities. We give them great acclaim and pay them huge amounts of money for acting like someone they are not. Horace Brandenberger never had to act like he was someone else because he was grounded in the land, and he set his compass by the harmony he saw in all living things. He answered when America's greatest generation called him to serve, and all of us are better for it. I always called him on Veterans' Day each year to tell him how much I appreciated what he had done for our country. When Veterans' Day comes this year, I will be thinking of him.

JANUARY 27, 2006

You may come to understand why a particular person does not measure up in a crisis; you may even come to look upon that person with compassion, but you do rejoice whenever you meet someone whose character is sterling; even in the greatest of stress, it remains the same. We came to refer to it as integrity.
—Larry Zellers[19]

Last evening, we met with a church group to view a marvelous film about the life of German theologian Dietrich Bonhoeffer.[20] Once again, I was deeply moved by this man's courage and his abiding faith. At the age of fourteen, young Dietrich shocked his affluent, but religiously indifferent, family by announcing his intention to become a theologian. Among Bonhoeffer's family were acclaimed historians, physicians, and physicists, and some of them thought he was selling himself short by entering the ministry. Despite family pressures to do otherwise, he pursued his studies with zeal and finished his doctorate in 1929 at the age of twenty-three. His brilliance and scholarly work gave him the opportunity to teach at renowned universities in the United States and Germany, but at heart he was a minister of the gospel.

The time of his ascendancy in the ranks of theologians loosely paralleled the rise of Adolf Hitler in Nazi Germany. While a large number of his colleagues in Germany looked the other way or refused to acknowledge what Hitler was doing, Bonhoeffer spoke out against the injustices he saw developing. He viewed the national frenzy being generated by the Nazis as a blueprint for disaster and declared that the church should have only one Fuehrer, and it was not Adolph Hitler. Through his writings and travel, he hoped to awaken the world to the Jewish persecutions in Germany. He was also actively involved in efforts to smuggle Jews out of the country.

Though he was urged by some theologians to remain silent, he openly defied Nazi edicts from the pulpit. In time he learned that his life, and possibly the lives of his family, were endangered. For a brief period, he left the country and lived in New York. Here his body was safe, but his mind was tormented, for he continued to hear of the atrocities in his native land. From New York he wrote, "I have come to the conclusion that I made a mistake in coming to America....I shall have no right to take part in the restoration of Christian life in Germany after the war unless I share the trials of this time with my people."[21]

Little did he know when he sailed from New York Harbor in the summer of 1939 that a world war would be under way when he reached his homeland. Once home, Bonhoeffer used his extensive international contacts to support the resistance movement. He also worked with others hoping to secure Allied support for an overthrow of the Nazi regime, but all efforts were rebuffed by Allied officials who insisted on an unconditional surrender. Nevertheless, Bonhoeffer continued his work in the resistance, supported efforts to get Jews out of the country and eventually became linked with those who wanted to assassinate Hitler. In 1943 Bonhoeffer was arrested and imprisoned. In 1945 he was transferred to an extermination camp near Flossemberg where, on Hitler's orders, he was hanged a few weeks before the Allied liberation of the city. Today, a small plaque on the tree from which he was hung says, "Dietrich Bonhoeffer, a witness to Jesus Christ among his brethren."[22] Four other members of his family also lost their lives to the Nazis.

JANUARY 28, 2006

Dietrich Bonhoeffer has been on my mind almost continually for the past two days. What was there about this man that caused him to live such an extraordinary life? Where did he summon the courage that enabled him to stand in the face of tyranny? In some respects, his sheltered life of privilege did little to prepare him for the chaos that erupted in Nazi Germany. Many of those around him supported the nationalistic endeavors of the Third Reich. Neither the Christian nor the Catholic churches, in the beginning, took aggressive stands against Nazi persecutions of Jews and other groups within Germany. In fact, senior ministers who supported Hitler encouraged Bonhoeffer to "let this thing be." But Bonhoeffer heard things others did not want to hear, and saw things others did not want to see.

In the film about Bonhoeffer's life, there is a vivid scene in which individuals burned books deemed undesirable by the Nazis. For me, the book burnings have always been a consummate reminder of what happens when people fear the truth. On a trip to the University of Texas when I was twelve years old, the UT Tower cast a spell over me that still exists today. High on the western summit of the tower is inscribed, "You shall know the truth and the truth shall make you free." I cannot say today what caused me to pause and reflect on those words that day, but it was a powerful experience. In the intervening years whenever I walked the campus, if only for a moment, I went to the west side.

A good part of my life was spent on university campuses, and I have had the pleasure of knowing some incredibly bright people. I came to know what it meant to sit at the feet of the masters, for they taught me things I could not have learned in any other setting. I also knew some people in higher education who were rather strange. They challenged most conventional thinking and didn't seem to care about what others thought about their lifestyles. I often wondered on what planet they were born. In spite of their constant pontification and confrontational attitudes, I enjoyed being around these people. If nothing else, they forced me to defend the truth as I knew it. In that regard, they were necessary parts of my education.

Today on many university campuses there are student groups committed to making others aware of the evils associated with the teachings of certain professors. Most of these groups are linked to the extreme religious right, but whether they are on the left or the right makes no difference; what they are doing is wrong. If our principles and beliefs cannot withstand a challenge, then they are built on a foundation of sand. In effect, these groups are saying that people cannot think for themselves. They reject the notion that anyone should be taught anything other than that which reflects their own narrow view of the world, and in so doing they become the new "book burners." The climate they seek to create is the same one that produced Martin Luther,

Galileo, and Rosa Parks. In the end, the truth always stands on its own, and it does set us free.

I think Dietrich Bonhoeffer believed this and that is why he had to do what he did. If we search deep within ourselves and if we have the courage to sail the right course, there can be something of Dietrich Bonhoeffer in each of us.

FEBRUARY 8, 2006

When I was told I had ALS I was deeply saddened, but I have never been afraid. That is, not until now. I still do not think I fear dying, although I know no one can say this with certainty until he or she gets there. My right hand continues to go on me in a rapid fashion and that brings me terror unlike anything I have ever known. When it is gone I will be totally dependent on others and that is a burden I cannot place on Veleda. My hope and my prayer is that I can hold out until Chad, Amy, and the grandsons move here so that I can share a brief time with them. After that, the place for me will be in nursing care. My desires on this will be challenged, but there are some things you know you must do.

FEBRUARY 10, 2006

Man is rich in terms of the number of things he can leave alone.—Henry David Thoreau[23]

I often think about a story a friend of mine, Hal, who worked for the Atomic Energy Commission of New Mexico, once told me. One day while walking near the missile range, he discovered a coyote caught in a steel trap. When the coyote saw Hal, he immediately began snarling and flashing his razor-sharp teeth in defiance. From every indication the coyote had put forth a valiant effort to escape, but the iron jaws of the trap refused to yield its prey. Near exhaustion, he watched the intruder with a wary interest.

Hal never told me how he did it, but he went about the rather dubious task of freeing the coyote. Eventually, he was able to set the animal free without suffering injury himself.

When the animal was free, Hal stepped away in anticipation of a mad rush to freedom. To his amazement the coyote continued to lie where he had been trapped. Hal knew the coyote was still mobile because of the energy and the range of motion he had exhibited during Hal's efforts to open the trap. He left the animal in the place where he had found him.

The next day, with his curiosity at a heightened level, Hal returned to the place where he had left the coyote. There he found the coyote dead on the exact spot where he had been set free the day before. Hal to this day maintains that the coyote died because he never believed he was free.

Sometimes in life we become ensnared in traps from which we could escape, but we choose not to do so. In reality these traps are self-imposed, but we cling to them as if they were immovable objects. A case in point may be the professional position we sometimes think we must have in order to be successful. Too many times I have seen individuals chasing high positions that ultimately bring them nothing but an enormous mortgage payment, a troubled spirit, and high blood pressure. I know about this, for I spent time in my life chasing that dragon.

There is nothing wrong with ambition, but there is something wrong with spending your life trying to measure up to other people's standards for success. The only person in life you can really please is the only person in the world you have control over, that person each of us sees in the mirror every morning. I have known CEOs, senators, hippies, entrepreneurs, professors, housewives, and custodians who were content with their lives. Conversely, I have known people in each of those groups who were wretched and mad at the world. I think that, by and large, their misery came from the fact that they permitted someone else to define success for them.

Other people sometimes choose to be trapped in relationships that strip them of their dignity and self-respect. I saw this happen so many times with high school and university students who would do anything to be accepted as part of the crowd. This was particularly the case with some young ladies who measured their self-worth by the status and popularity of their boyfriends. (Yes, I know this is sexist language but at this stage in life, I don't really care what the watchdogs think.) No matter how abusive or condescending a boyfriend might be, he remained a link to status the young lady felt she could not get on her own. This phenomenon is not unique to young ladies; young men sometimes seek the same kind of destructive relationship with girlfriends. Whatever the case, nothing good comes from trying to live life through someone else.

In the movie *Legends of the Fall*, actor Brad Pitt played an unscrupulous character who made life miserable for those who loved him. Everyone around him thought they could change him, but the truth was he did not want to be changed. Late in the movie, one character described him as "the rock we all broke ourselves against."[24] I see so many people break themselves against someone else because they spend a lifetime thinking they can change an irresponsible spouse, sibling, child, friend, or colleague. Too often, because the behavior does not change, the concerned person may even come to see herself or himself as the cause of the problem. I am not saying a positive relationship cannot change an irresponsible person, but I am saying you're working with long odds. Unless a person truly wants to change, you cannot will them to change. If given the choice, invest your time, energy, trust, and love in someone else.

In the end the traps we choose to let snare us are often much more destructive than those we spend a lifetime trying to avoid.

FEBRUARY 14, 2006

The first purple martins arrived today. They left eight months ago for some destination in South America, probably Argentina or Brazil. No one seems to know exactly what routes they take for their annual migration, but it is difficult for me to imagine a bird that small surviving the horrendous flight to another continent. Whenever they arrive it is a time for celebration and rejoicing, for they bring so much joy to our lives. Their antics in claiming apartment space in the martin house and their acrobatic maneuvers in flight provide endless entertainment for Veleda and me. Their incessant chatter, which begins with the break of day, is a constant reminder of life and living things. We will celebrate their arrival with a glass of wine on the porch this evening. In the past they have never arrived here before the third week in February. I guess they knew I needed them to come early this year.

FEBRUARY 20, 2006

God is the friend of silence.
See how nature—trees, flowers, grass—grows in silence;
see the stars, the moon and the sun, how they move in silence…
We need silence to be able to touch souls.—Mother Teresa[25]

Sometimes seemingly insignificant events become very significant with time. In the fall of 2000, an overnight thunderstorm brought rain to our parched land. I got up shortly after daylight and with our Kelpie dog, Belle, by my side, I walked through the damp grass into the pasture. It was one of those unforgettable mornings we have come to appreciate. The air had been washed clean by the rain. The strong winds that had thrashed the landscape earlier no longer breathed. As I walked along the rock fence, I could hear ahead of me the rush of water that the night before had been in the sky but now made its way to the craggy pathway of Panther Creek. Patches of fog shrouded much of the landscape around me, but I could maintain my bearings by listening to the sound of the creek ahead and following the slope of the land. My rubber boots gave me passage through the tributaries running toward the creek; Belle, ahead of me, alternately splashed and swam her way through the water.

The most beautiful spot on the ranch is a place we call the Kettle. This place is situated in the neck of a funnel that drains the main body of Panther Creek and several tributaries. Amid limestone formations twenty feet high on both sides, the water enters a narrow cut where it tumbles unrestrained over ledges and crevices into a shallow pool below. On this day we walked to the head of the Kettle and gazed at the rushing waters about and below us. In the pool below, where the water sleeps, I could see a form moving in the rising fog. Belle, too, saw the movement and stood transfixed by my side.

Moments later a white-tailed buck could be seen drinking from the creek. He knew we were there but made no effort to run. Eventually, having drunk his fill, he slowly walked back into the fog. Maybe he knew that on this day and in this place no bad thing could happen. There were no sounds here but nature's sounds. Later there would be air traffic, pickups driving on the county road, and distant chainsaws spoiling the silence. In that moment, however, there were no intruders here except for me, and I quietly moved back upstream leaving the silence but taking the memory.

FEBRUARY 21, 2006

Work is either fun or drudgery. It depends on your attitude. I like fun.—Colleen C. Barrett, CEO of Southwest Airlines[26]

When I was fourteen years old I got my first job washing dishes in a restaurant on Lake Buchanan. The job paid fifty cents an hour, and by the end of the summer I had saved enough money to pay eighty dollars for a 1942 Ford V-8. The "little miss" in the engine the car dealer told me about turned out to be a cracked head, which meant the car didn't run very long. Despite this imperfection, when I had my car loaded down with friends driving around town on nineteen-cents-a-gallon gasoline, I thought I was behind the wheel of a Rolls-Royce. Thus began an addiction to automobiles that lasted throughout my teen years.

The next summer I began working for sixty cents an hour in a lime plant where my dad was a foreman. At sixty cents an hour, plus time and a half for overtime, I was really in the money. My dad was a man of few words but when he talked, I listened. On the way to work that first day he said, "Jimmy, you need to remember today that you are the boss's son." I guess that's the only thing he ever told me about working, but the message was clear; everybody would be watching me to see if I pulled my own weight.

Dad could read emotional fields pretty well, and sometimes I saw flashes of brilliance in his leadership. A case in point had to do with his first day on the job. He was the first plant foreman in a company with 95 percent Hispanic workers. For good reasons the workforce was very suspicious of all managers, and Anglos in particular. Dad knew this and that is why the first thing he did was to go to a longtime employee named Adrian Zamarripa, who was the informal leader among the workers. He told "Mr. Sam," as he was called, that he wanted him to teach him everything he knew about running the plant.

Dad could not have made a smarter tactical move because Mr. Sam was one of the most respected men I ever knew. He had four sons working at the plant who played a major role in the culture of the organization. His grandson, Philippi, to this day is one of my closest friends. Mr. Sam taught my dad a great deal about management and both of us about class. Dad had a good relationship with most of the men at work, and eventually they gave him the nickname Zancudo, which in Spanish means "mosquito," or in Dad's case, "little man with a big bite."

In that first summer, I worked on the docks loading boxcars and trucks with fifty-pound sacks of hydrated lime and sometimes ninety-pound bags of quicklime. My working partner was Lena Amaro, better known as Uncle Lena. I never knew how old he was because he could not speak English, but I would guess he was closer to eighty than seventy. He came to the United States, I was told, because earlier he had made a wrong decision about which revolutionary party to support in Mexico. Though we shared no common language, he communicated to me in a masterful way. He was one of the most genteel people I have ever known. Later he would be the model for the character Enrique in my novel *Companions of the Blest*.

The first morning on the job, Uncle Lena and I were assigned to load eight hundred sacks of lime on a trailer truck. My dad's words were still ringing in my ears, so I set out to show everyone how hard I could work. In the beginning I was throwing sacks in place with reckless abandon. Though less tidy, my rows were always completed first. Uncle Lena worked at an unvarying rhythmic rate, stacking his sacks meticulously. By the time we finished with a load, I had easily loaded the most sacks. When truck number one was completed, we immediately began another. This time I loaded fewer sacks but still more than Uncle Lena. By the middle of the afternoon, Uncle Lena was still loading sacks at his usual rate. I was exhausted, barely able to take care of my side of the truck. Uncle Lena knew something about pacing that I came to better understand that day.

By any measure, the working conditions at the lime plant were terrible. The ownership of the company demonstrated little or no regard for employees. During our time there, three men were killed and one was maimed for life. The plant was eventually closed down by the EPA for violations of air-quality regulations. The constant dust settled onto and into everything, including eyes and lungs. If someone got quicklime onto his sweaty skin, it would begin eating away at the flesh. Even in 100-degree-plus weather we had to wear long-sleeved shirts and bandannas around our necks to keep quicklime dust away from our skin. I will always believe that conditions there caused the disability and eventual deaths of numerous workers, including my father.

I was never much of a union man, but having worked there I can easily see how the militant labor movement in this country began. The workforce in the company, established in the 1800s, originally consisted largely of Mexican immigrants. Given the abysmal working conditions described above, it would seem that workers would quickly move on to other things, but the company had its ways. At one time a company store existed there, and I am told workers were paid in tokens redeemable at the company store. The company also built houses next to the plant that it rented to workers. Given the fact that the company was the employer, grocer, and landlord for all practical purposes, the workers lived in a fiefdom. Until the 1950s their children, if they attended school, went to the "Mexican school" where conditions and expectations were dismal. Most of them had no transportation, so there was no way to really get away from the company's control, and the same families worked there year after year. By the time I came there, the store had closed down and most of the houses remaining were little more than shanties. During the hot and dry summer months, lime from the hydrator and dust from the powder-dry roads settled onto everything in the surrounding area like a winter snowfall. Those living nearest to the kilns walked from their front doors into a three-inch layer of lime dust, which the winds blew to and fro, often through their open windows.

As bad as things were at the plant, it was a great school for me. I benefited enormously from what I learned about how people choose to cope with difficult environments, and my love for the Hispanic culture could have evolved from no better setting. Although today OSHA would quickly shut down an operation such as that, the men there refused to let the dreadful working conditions break their spirit. Despite the difficult circumstances, most of them spent a lot of time laughing and teasing one another. Later when they began to tease me, I realized I had passed through a rite of passage of some sort. Even when the lime dust was so thick you could not see where he was, I could often hear Red Martinez singing while he bagged lime for the pallets. These men taught me a great deal about love of family, and despite their humble circumstances, they never lost their pride. It was through them I came to appreciate authentic Tex-Mex cuisine. Sometimes, if I were lucky, I would pass by where John Zamarripa worked just as he was putting flour tortillas on a piece of metal next to the kilns. Filled with refried beans, a strip of bacon, chopped jalapenos, and sometimes fresh nopolitos, his homemade tortillas were the best I have ever eaten. I have, without success, tried to replicate them several times. I fix a pretty good plate of nopolitos, though, and when I do, I think back to that place.

I did lose some of my youth there, however. While most of the boys my age enjoyed their Saturdays and Sundays doing what teenagers do, I spent my time working at the lime plant. I didn't have to do this, but I wanted a succession of cars (1942 Ford, 1948 Plymouth, 1949 Oldsmobile, 1951 Ford, 1953 Mercury) that resulted in perpetual car payments during my high school years. Looking back, I now know that the cars weren't worth it, but life is always viewed through the windows of the time.

Later when it came time to go to college, I chose architecture as a major. I made that decision based on a single aptitude test and because I knew it would please my dad. I really had no interest in architecture other than it sounded like an impressive major. It took me a while to realize that what I wanted to do was to teach. My heroes at school had always been coaches, and later at the university I would add professors to that list.

My first job as a teacher and coach in Fredericksburg, Texas, paid $4,500 a year, and my last as a college president paid me much more than I was worth. I never regretted my decision to become a teacher. Not all of that thirty-five-year period was pleasant, but most of it was an enormously fulfilling experience. I once heard Sandy Koufax, the Hall of Fame pitcher for the Los Angeles Dodgers, say, "I thank God every day that I have the opportunity to be a Major League pitcher." I felt the same way about the opportunity I had to become a university professor. I regularly told my graduate students I would teach for nothing if someone would pay my bills and buy the groceries. I'm not sure they believed me, but I hope they understood the compliment I was trying to pay them.

Of all the lessons I learned during my working days, I am not sure but what the most important occurred at the lime plant. The opportunity to work with those men who had so little, but found so much, had a profound effect on my life. We can find joy and meaning in most anything we do if we are up for the search.

FEBRUARY 23, 2006

If one can believe the polls, most Americans disagree with the way George Bush is running the country. Some predict a Democratic takeover in Congress in the next election. I was particularly amused today to hear a strategist for the Democratic Party talk about what the party should do in preparation for the fall elections. In response to a commentator's question regarding what issues the Democrats would run on, the strategist said they are going to continue to remind the American people of the terrible job the Republicans have done. "But what about your own agenda?" the commentator asked. The strategist responded, "We don't need to lay out an agenda; all that will do is just give the opposition a platform to run against us."

If this is the gutless strategy the Democrats intend to employ, they will lose again just as they have done in the last several elections. I have never trusted people who spend all their time telling me what they won't do or for that matter, what they do not believe. I have to believe the American people, as bad as things are, will not vote for any party that has no vision for the future. Long ago when I was his graduate student, Dr. Barry B. Thompson, the former chancellor of the Texas A&M University System, told me, "A leader without a vision is nothing more than a bureaucrat." Bureaucrats don't lead, they just react. We need much more than that now.

Chapter 4
The Leader Is the Keeper of the Dream

When corporate boards are asked what type of CEOs they want to employ, they usually talk first about trust, honor, honesty, and other matters of character. Somewhere in the conversation visionary leadership will generally be discussed. Boards want leaders who envision a pathway to excellence. Most leaders want to leave behind visionary legacies, but if the U.S. presidency is any indicator, historians award the title of visionary to very few.

Being at the right place at the right time, with a good idea, does not necessarily make a person a visionary. It could make one rich and famous, but visions of substance, visions that take organizations to world-class performance are much more complex than a single person's bright idea. In fact, Jim Collins's longitudinal study of extraordinary corporate leaders found no significant link between world-class performance and the fact that the leader was a "visionary."[1] That did not mean, however, that their *organizations* were without vision.

Visions that change lives, visions that capture the hearts of people in the organization, visions that endure are more than words on a page from a strategic plan gathering dust on a shelf somewhere. Authentic visions are derived from compelling needs identified by the organization and by passions within the organization for fulfilling those needs. Jim Kouzes, who wrote *The Leadership Challenge*, found that visionary leaders chart courses into the future by igniting passions.[2] Cosmetics queen Mary Kay Ash is a master at generating passion through organizational pep rallies. Not all organizational visions are formulated in a Mary Kay emotional frenzy, but the principle is the same. People have to believe the vision is taking them to a better place, or they will not commit to the journey. *The leader's role is not necessarily to be the architect of the vision but to create an environment that encourages a vision to flow from the hearts and minds of the people in the organization.* How this process effectively evolves within organizations is contingent on a number of factors. Some common practices found within many visionary organizations follow.

Visit the Mountaintop

Who is to say where great dreams originate? They may occur within the hustle and bustle of the workplace, but that is unlikely. Most conscientious people in the workplace are too consumed with the pressures of the moment to give serious thought to dreaming dreams of great things. The matter is further complicated by the fact that some leaders believe visioning experiences are a waste of organizational time. This kind of thinking produces a rudderless ship sailing chaotic seas, with no destination or points of reference.

Of all organizations, families probably spend the least amount of time visioning their futures. There may be visions for individuals in the family, such as college for the children, but seldom do families sit down together and envision what they want to be and how they want to direct their future.

In order to think at our highest levels, we must break the routine. Moses went to the mountaintop to hear God's message; most of us, upon reaching a summit, have been inspired by the view below. It would be nice to take the leadership team, the church council, or the family for a soul-searching experience in Glacier National Park, but that is not practical for most organizations. I think visioning is more likely to occur in a setting conducive to creative thinking where there are minimal interruptions. Sometimes we have to create our own mountaintop experiences. The critical role for leaders of organizations and families is to regularly bring members together to dream dreams of great things and possibilities for the future. Given creative leadership, an air for open discussion, and a place of solitude, a mountaintop experience can be created on the Mississippi Delta.

You Cannot Steal a Vision

We live in a copycat world. When great things happen to organizations, they immediately become the focal point for those who seek to profit from others' innovations. *Pirating* has moved from the high seas to the high-rise office complex. While some companies with look-alike products may pirate their way to profitability, you cannot pirate a vision. The best way to create an organizational "crash and burn" site is to download another organization's vision. If the vision belongs to someone else, it can never be a thing of passion for employees. If the vision belongs to someone else, it will not meet the organization's needs, because no two organizations are alike.

Listen to Others

Leaders I have respected over the years were known more for the questions they asked than the answers they provided. Socrates shaped intellectual thought through the ages by posing questions that challenged others to higher levels of thinking. TD Industries and Southwest Airlines have made significant profits by constantly posing vision questions to their employees.[3] When leaders ask subordinates for an opinion, they are not only seeking information, but they are also affirming the subordinates' worth to the organization. Each is a powerful medicine. Great leaders believe in the power of collective wisdom, for they know the best thinking comes from ground level and not necessarily from the thin air at the top of the organizational pyramid. That is why some companies today draw their vision more from what their customers tell them than they do from organizational think tanks.

Once a vision has been identified, *the most important role for the leader is to protect the vision.* All quality visions involve change, and change is going to make some people in the organization uncomfortable. Leaders know there can be no change without pain. When Anne Sullivan began working with young Helen Keller, she had a vision that this blind and deaf child, prone to uncontrollable temper tantrums, would learn to read, write, and speak. Helen Keller's parents had similar expectations, but they could not accept the significant changes in their lives that Anne Sullivan demanded. Only when Helen Keller was removed from the overprotective environment of her home could progress be made. Anne Sullivan never lost sight of the vision, but she had to make some people very uncomfortable for the dream to be realized.[4]

Within most organizations, there are a small number of people reluctant to believe in possibilities. They are not forward-thinkers, preferring instead to maintain the status quo or move back to old models. This is not to say that they do not have ideas worth considering, but if allowed to control the agenda, they can destroy the dream. *Failure forecasters* are usually vocal, and they demand a disproportionate share of the leader's time. They are the people leaders stay awake at night worrying about, and they often make for an uncomfortable drive to work in the morning. I have seen leaders, in particular young leaders, worry themselves into a frenzy because they cannot make negative people happy. The truth is that those in the organization who thrive on negativity will probably never be satisfied. Oftentimes these individuals are miserable in their personal lives and need little prompting to try to create a culture of misery within the organization. Visionary leaders know the best return on their investment of time will come from forward-thinkers with a passion to move the organization to a higher level.[5]

I have spent considerable time over the past years interviewing employees from industry leader Southwest Airlines. One way Southwest seeks to protect its vision is through the hiring process.[6] The company's motto is to "hire for attitude, and train for success." Regardless of their technical expertise, applicants must have positive attitudes and be forward-thinkers, or they will not be asked to join the Southwest team.

Another motto strongly supported by company executives is: "The customer is not always right." Southwest respects the integrity of its employees and will not force them to work in a demeaning environment. In that organizational culture, employees are more likely to accept and protect the vision.

In every aspect of our lives, we monitor what we value. Concerned parents know where their children are, successful coaches look after athletes on and off the field, and effective ministers watch over congregations. Leaders who value a vision make every effort to monitor it. Visions die quickly when leadership fails to identify benchmarks, celebrate successes, and make necessary adjustments. We enliven visions when we make them a part of board agendas, staff meetings, and community gatherings.

Visionary leaders who take organizations to great heights know it is much easier to create than to protect visions. Authentic visionaries are characterized by their unrelenting pursuit of the vision, for they know ultimately that "the leader is the keeper of the dream."[7]

March 12, 2006

Of the people I have known, I enjoy being around storytellers more than all others. Storytellers feed our spirits with insights and stories of the human condition that we can get from no other source. There are fewer and fewer storytellers today because too often we choose not to invest our time in other people. Storytellers come from all walks of life. Unaffected by status, their uniqueness evolves from observations of life's experiences that are largely ignored by others.

One storyteller I'll always remember was James Doss of Weatherford, Texas. James was probably the wealthiest man I have ever known, but he never flaunted his status. A world traveler, on each of his trips he brought back at least one story worth hearing. He delivered his stories with such exuberance and joy that it was impossible not to listen to him. His gut-wrenching laughter was infectious, and I was never around him more than a few moments without my mood improving. I don't recall him ever telling me a story in which he was the hero, but he did look for and find heroes wherever he went.

Another unforgettable storyteller was Richard "Dick" Moore, the proprietor of Barnard's Mill in Glen Rose, Texas. A decorated World War II gunnery officer who served on a B-24 bomber, Dick was an attorney by profession, but he spent considerable time ranching and collecting art. Late in life he restored the historic Barnard's Mill. The mill, situated on the Paluxy River, was built when the Texas frontier lay to the east. Over the years it served as a trading post, fortress, gristmill, and home for the Barnard family. It was in this place that we enjoyed memorable evenings sitting beside the enormous fireplace, sipping wine and enjoying good stories. When the time was right, Dick would begin playing the piano and this usually led to his singing a medley of World War II drinking songs. I think he was born on center stage, and we happily granted him that honor. We came to know him as a marvelous storyteller who had lived long enough to know much about the joys, horrors, disappointments, and victories of America's greatest generation.

One of his best stories involves the legendary Houston attorney, Percy Foreman. It seems one day Mr. Foreman was interviewing prospective jurors in an aggressive fashion, and with one particular gentleman he was somewhat curt. The prospective juror in short order was offended by the manner of questioning and a confrontational dialogue developed. Foreman would ask him, "What do you think about this?" or "What do you think about that?" Each time, the juror would reply in some caustic fashion. Finally Foreman asked, "And what do you think about me?" Without hesitation the man replied, "I think you are a worthless son of a bitch!" Without missing a beat, Foreman turned to the judge and matter-of-factly said, "Your honor, I will take this juror. He is an excellent judge of character."

Another memorable storyteller was Floyd Coleman, who occasionally worked as a day laborer for Veleda's father. A descendent of slaves, Floyd and his wife, Rosie, lived in a run-down house, under which a large assortment of cats and dogs resided. When I met him, he was well into his sixties, but he carried his lean six-foot-two frame with the grace of a person much younger. By today's standards Floyd would have been labeled as economically deprived or underprivileged. Whatever label anyone would have wanted to bestow on him would have been rejected by Floyd. He had too much pride to accept another person's designation. Yet if you wanted information on the weather, hound dogs, veterinary science, Levi Garrett snuff, heaven and hell, or "the mark of a man," Floyd had some answers. I listened to him with great interest as, hour after hour, he would spin yarns from earlier times. Fortunately Jeff, Chad, and their cousins had a brief opportunity to learn from Floyd before he died.

In a lifetime most of us accumulate knowledge to some degree or another. A smaller number of people with knowledge actually have wisdom. I don't know all that is involved in moving from knowledge to wisdom, but I think a part of it has to do with how much attention we pay to storytellers we have known.

MARCH 13, 2006

Over the years I have particularly enjoyed stories about children. Children need to hear stories from us, but stories from children inevitably keep our moral compass pointed in the right direction. They are the most honest people I know, for they have not yet learned to be otherwise. Much more so than adults, they believe in possibilities and therefore see a less cluttered world. Three stories of children follow.

When I was president of Weatherford College and the fiftieth anniversary of the Normandy invasion rolled around, we decided to host a symposium featuring World War II veterans. There were a large number of veterans in the community and some of them had been prisoners of war. Our hope was to capture on tape stories from these American heroes that would become a part of our oral history archives.

We correctly projected that several of the veterans would want to participate in the program. What we did not anticipate was the emotion that soon engulfed the speakers. The private hell that many of these men had known fifty years earlier sprang forth again that day. The former POWs, in particular, spoke with extreme bitterness about the hardships they had faced and friends they had lost. I marveled at how any of them, in particular the one gentleman who had survived the Bataan Death March, were able to return to any semblance of normalcy in their lives. From their stories of hardships and torture, it was easy to see how they had come to feel the way they did about the former Axis powers.

I will never forget any of the stories told that day, but the one I think about most often was John Johnson's story. John, an instructor at the college, was the last speaker on the emotion-laden agenda. He never talked much about his combat experiences, but I know he was engaged in some of the most vicious battles of the war. When he began to speak, he talked about his unit's march across Germany and its advance on the city of Ruhpolding, a place decimated by war, and with a civilian population desperate for food and medical attention.

Somewhere in the streets of the city, he was besieged by hungry children begging for something to eat. He shared with them all that he had to eat, which was only a few chocolate bars. He talked of the look in the children's eyes and the effect their penetrating stares had on him. Before him were the descendents of the people he had been trying to kill, yet among them he saw nothing but innocent, fearful children who had forgotten how to smile. He concluded his remarks by saying, "For me, the war ended in that moment."

Not long after the September 11, 2001, attack on New York City, Veleda and I traveled to the Mediterranean. Among the planned stops on our itinerary was Istanbul, Turkey. We had never visited an Islamic country, so given the fact that our troops were involved in major military operations in Afghanistan, we had some concern about going there at that particular time. The lure of this place, though, which has played such an important part in the story of civilization, was compelling. I shall never forget the moment we sailed into the harbor and had our first view of the city. Before us on the hillside stood the Chapel of St. Sophia, built by Roman Emperor Constantine, and also the Blue Mosque, a holy shrine of the Muslim world. These two sites played enormous roles in the development of two world religions in a city historically often besieged by both East and West.

The ambience of the city exceeded all of our expectations. The people were incredibly cordial to us, and wherever we went I felt as though we were on some part of history's stage. The only unexpected turn of events came when Veleda informed me that a fundamental purpose for our visit to the city, and perhaps a hidden agenda for the trip from the start, was the purchase of a Persian rug. Sometime later, a local merchant made me promise that I would "tell no other person about the one-time-only deal" he was willing to make me for the rug we have in our living room today.

As we were winding down the day, we walked through a small park. We had been there for only a brief time when a young group of elementary school boys and girls in their immaculate school uniforms arrived. They were a handsome group, to say the least. They quickly charmed most of the adults in our group. Eventually one of the boys came up to me. Though we shared no common language, his dancing eyes and bright smile begged for attention. I reached out to shake hands with him and he lifted his small hand to mine. Instead of a conventional handshake, I used a "jive shake" taught to me by some of our college basketball players. The young boy immediately broke into laughter and his friend eagerly stepped forward, expecting equal treatment.

In short order, each of the other thirty or so boys and girls got in line to shake hands. I was about halfway down the line when our tour guide summoned us to the bus. Though I knew I would face the wrath of the awaiting tour group, there was no way I was going to leave the magic of that moment. Eventually I shook hands with the last little girl in the line and made my way back to accusatory stares from my fellow travelers.

I was once asked to speak to a leadership conference in El Paso, Texas. Whenever I was on the road I always tried to find time and a good place to jog. Most cities located on rivers have recreational areas near the river, so in El Paso I headed toward the Río Grande. I walked for several minutes in the direction I thought I should go, but to no avail. Somewhat later, I came upon two gentlemen sitting on the curb drinking something from a bottle in a brown paper bag. I soon learned they could speak no English, so in my limited Spanish I asked them about how to get to the river. Eventually they understood what I wanted to know and pointed me in another direction.

As I walked away from them, perhaps as an omen of what was about to occur, one of the men said, *"Vaya con Dios,"* in other words, "God be with you." I soon found the river but no jogging trail. It was obvious from the sordid pathways that there was a great deal of traffic on the east side of the river so I turned right and headed upstream. A few moments later I startled a group of men lying in the shade of the underbrush. You didn't need to be a seasoned river runner to see that these men, who were waiting for the sun to go down, were unsettled by my presence. I accelerated up a pathway that ended abruptly about one hundred yards later at the bottom of a steep embankment next to the interstate. I was not particularly interested in trying to climb the steep embankment and cross the interstate in my jogging suit, but the thought of going back through the under-brush on the trail was not appealing, either. At that point I noticed a twenty-four-inch water main that spanned the river and connected two countries. On the opposite shore I could see children delicately balancing themselves as they walked the water main. Given my options at that point, I decided to go to Mexico. "Surely," I thought, "I can find my way down to the bridge and a return to the east side of the river."

I began walking across the water main. About three-quarters of the way across the river it occurred to me that where I was going, a person in a navy blue jogging suit might stand out in the crowd. These thoughts were reinforced as more and more chil-dren began to gather around the other end of the water main. There was quite a contingent waiting for me when I arrived in Juarez, Mexico. One young boy who was the leader of my recep-tion committee began to talk to me rapidly in Spanish. The only thing I could understand from what he said was, "¿Cómo se llama?" which means "What is your name?" I told him my name was Santiago, which is "Jimmy" in Spanish. He told me his name was Juisto. The exchange of names seemed to verify with the group that I was worthy of acceptance. Accompanied by ten or so children, I then began a walk to nowhere in the barrios of Juarez. Needless to say, we created quite a spectacle. The children talked to everyone we met, and while I could not understand all they were saying, I'm sure the message must have been "look what we found down by the river."

I had previously been to Mexico several times and twice traveled to the interior. I thought I knew all there was to know about Mexican poverty, but I learned that day that I was mis-taken. The houses on the mud-ridden streets would have been substandard in any Third World country. One disfigured man emerged from a dwelling made from refrigerator boxes. At another place, a family was gathered around their home located in a ravine covered by four pieces of rusty corrugated tin. It was impossible for an adult to stand up in the structure, whose front entrance was covered by burlap bags. Outside the front door was a five-gallon can of water that likely served all the water needs for the family. There were other places too numerous to mention that I remember from that day.

It did not take me long to conclude that in the barrios, most streets look alike and that I was about to be seriously lost. My entourage was also dwindling because some of the parents, with scornful looks, called their children back out of the streets. Even Juisto abandoned our group in pursuit of a mongrel dog that did not want to be caught. With patience and a lot of luck, I alone retraced my trail back to the point of origin in Mexico. I was about to begin my high-wire journey back across the river when there was Juisto again. This time he was alone, but I could hear other boys playing in the willows behind him. I waved to him and said good-bye; he didn't say anything but he did smile just before he dashed off into the undergrowth. On the other side of the river, I climbed the steep embankment, and with some spectacular broken-field running, made my way safely across the interstate.

I often reflect on this children's trilogy from three different decades on three different continents. If they survived the war, the children John Johnson met would be about my age. There is a possibility that they spent the bulk of their lives living under communism. If they were not subjected to communism, others like them were. I dare not speculate about what communism brought them, but I do know what it took from them. Communism, as it existed in Eastern Europe, survived on terror and lies about the past, the present, and the future. It quickly took from young people the innocence of youth and sought to program their minds to serve the state.

Juisto, and the other children along the banks of the Río Grande in Juarez, are approaching thirty. If Juisto is alive today, I hope he was able to escape the barrios. The odds are he is still there. The deplorable conditions in the barrios continue to worsen despite one Mexican regime after another promising reforms that never occur. Some historians maintain the plight of the Mexican poor has changed very little since Hernando Cortes began his conquest of the Aztecs in 1519. Unfortunately, one pathway out of the barrios for young men is the illicit drug trade. Drug wars have made some unscrupulous individuals on both sides of the border immensely wealthy and have made Juarez the murder capital of this hemisphere. Americans are quick to berate Mexicans for criminal activity in their country. Yet we somehow see no correlation between the Saturday night recreational use of cocaine in a Manhattan high-rise and the fact that a young man like Juisto could be lying in a pool of blood on a dirty street in Juarez.

The children in Istanbul are now about to enter secondary school. I wonder what their fate will be. I dare not venture a guess, but in the back of my mind I keep thinking of the huge gulf that now exists between my faith and theirs. How did the children of Abraham manage to create a world now filled with so much hate and uncertainty? I am particularly disturbed by the fact that moderates in both the Muslim and Christian faiths have allowed fundamentalists, intolerant of beliefs other than their own, to exert enormous influence over religion. Within both faiths, these extremists ultimately hope to eliminate those who do not share their narrow view of the world.

As I think about children and our responsibility to them, I am often reminded of Matthew 25:40, in which Jesus said, "just as you did it to one of the least of these…you did it to me." By American standards, most of the world's children live in poverty. In fact, the number of poor children in the United States is growing at unprecedented rates. There is nothing inherently wrong in being poor; many of us grew up that way. But there is something profoundly wrong when poverty, as it does in so many countries, equates to malnutrition, disease, and early death. When people grow up in a miserable existence where they feel they have no options, a "culture of rage" can flourish. Ultimately the world is the loser.

Aᴘʀɪʟ 4, 2006

Other than the Bible, I do not think a must-read book has ever been written. There are, however, any number of books, both fiction and nonfiction, that can contribute to one's development and offer insights into the nature of the world in which we live. Some works of nonfiction that I believe have merit are:

- *The Autobiography of Benjamin Franklin*
- *The Autobiography of Mark Twain*
- *Goodbye to a River* by John Graves
- *John Adams* by David McCullough
- *Travels with Charlie* by John Steinbeck
- *Walden* by Henry David Thoreau
- *Adventures of a Texas Naturalist* by Roy Bedichek

Some works of fiction that I believe have extraordinary worth are:

- *The Time It Never Rained* by Elmer Kelton
- *The Old Man and the Sea* by Ernest Hemingway
- *Lonesome Dove* by Larry McMurtry
- *Red Sky at Morning* by Richard Bradford
- *The Little Shepherd of Kingdom Come* by John Fox
- *Huckleberry Finn* by Mark Twain

Aᴘʀɪʟ 12, 2006

I lift up my eyes to the hills. From whence will my help come? My help comes from the Lord, who made heaven and earth. —Psalm 121

I spend a part of every day sitting on the front porch looking to the west as the sun lightens or darkens the craggy surface of Cannon Mountain. It's not really a mountain; most people would describe it as a hill. Its character comes from a steep ascent from the mesquite flat below. The summit is 2,200 feet above sea level, and from it there is a grand view of the valley of the Llano to the north, and to the left some people say you can see all the way to West Texas. Our ranch house is to the east where the windmill pokes its head through a live-oak canopy. In a canyon on the south slope, my horse once bucked me onto a not very soft landing surface. I never lost the reins, but I sat there for a full ten minutes looking up at my horse and trying to put air back into lungs that seemed to have forgotten their purpose. Not wanting to concede any advantage to my horse, eventually I got back into the saddle and took the longest ride of my life back home. Two days later, when my manly pride succumbed to constant pain, I went to the doctor, who told me I had a separated shoulder and two cracked ribs.

The mountain is not on our property, but the three different ranchers who own a part of it have given us permission to go there. On more than one occasion Veleda and I went to a special place to drink wine and watch the day pass into the night. I wrote part of my novel there. I am told that years ago on the Fourth of July, Veleda's grandfather Jim Brandenberger would celebrate the occasion by throwing lit sticks of dynamite from the summit into the valley below. Just across the county road on the north side, the last mountain lion in the area was killed. In those days mountain lions were called panthers, and it was from that incident, I am told, that Panther Creek on our place got its name.

The steep surface of the mountainside chronicles the arrival of fall each year. The leaves on the Spanish oaks and sumacs that cling to life on a barren hillside turn a fiery red that rivals any landscape I have observed in the Northeast. As fall passes into winter, the leaves disappear and the trees stand there alone in their nakedness, waiting for the turn of the solstice to clothe them again. In the winter, when there is a heavy frost or the occasional ice storm, the rays of the morning sun illuminate the mountainside with a splendor that defies description.

One memory of the place I shall never forget occurred when two of Veleda's German cousins and their spouses visited us in 2004. All four of them spent part of their early life in a Communist concentration camp in what was then Yugoslavia. Their families lost all their possessions. Two of them saw their father shot by Communist sympathizers. In order to take the children's minds away from what they had experienced in the camps, each evening the mothers would bring the children together to sing. In time, the four of them formed a marvelous singing group with incredibly tight harmony. While they were with us, one morning before the heat of the day we decided to climb the mountain. It was an incredibly glorious day; the coolness of the night was still in the air and all around us the birds were singing. At the top of the mountain we gazed upon the valley below. It was at that point when the cousins spontaneously began singing "How Great Thou Art" in German. The beauty of their voices and the power in the message seemed to ring out from the summit to the expanse below. To hear these people, who had experienced so many hardships earlier in life, sing God's praises was an extraordinarily uplifting experience. I don't know that I had ever before felt any closer to my creator than I did in that moment.

As with the rest of the Hill Country, I suspect in time the summit of the mountain will be violated by the houses of millionaires who see it as nothing more than an extension of their power and money. I am grateful that our family has known something different, and that Cannon Mountain will always be a place of memories. If you go there at the right time of day and if you give all of yourself to the moment, it can be a sacred place.

APRIL 14, 2006

While living in a tent in Montana when I was nineteen years old, I came to enjoy classical music. That's not the way music appreciation usually develops, but for me it was probably the only way it could have occurred. That summer I began my second tour of duty as a firefighter with the U.S. Forest Service. In the interim between fires, our crew spent most of its time in the mountains clearing brush from the fire trails. We lived in tents about thirty-five miles from Thompson Falls, alongside a fast-flowing stream called Trout Creek.

After supper each evening we lay in our bunks, exhausted from both the day's trek into the high country and from eating too much food prepared by our exceptional camp cook. With the dimming of the day, we could hear Trout Creek rushing past our tents on its way to the Clark Fork of the Missouri River. It was a time of tranquility and reflection that I enjoyed immensely.

We had no electricity in the camp, but a guy in my tent named George Bogdon had a portable radio. Given our remote location, the radio would pick up only one station two states over in Spokane, Washington. At nine o'clock everyone perked up because that was when the "Lucky Logger Hour" played all of the hot rock 'n' roll songs of the day. From seven to eight, however, the time when we lay there alternating between periods of slumber and quiet conversation, the station played only classical music. The music matched the mood of the camp, and in time I came to appreciate it immensely. It was in that environment I first heard *Madame Butterfly*, which even today stirs my soul. I never became a classical music aficionado, but with dinner or in quiet times, I find the music of the ages most enjoyable.

George Bogdon was a genuine article. His parents were either dead or gone, and he lived mostly out of a cardboard box. The opportunity to work for the Forest Service each summer gave him not only room and board, but also the money to support his hunting and fishing habits. Most of the guys in our camps were college students enrolled in preprofessional programs of some kind. It would be an understatement to say that George didn't fit with this group made up largely of fraternity boys. The truth was that he did not want to fit into any group. When they moved our crew up to Trout Creek for the summer, I chose to live in the tent with George. His radio may have influenced my decision, but I think there was something else there, also. I never really got along all that well with fraternity boys. I thought then, and still believe now, that most fraternities are pompous organizations ultimately demeaning to individualism.

George taught me a great deal. He was an excellent fly fisherman, and he took me to some incredibly beautiful places to fish for brook trout and to share stories. He was also my introduction to the works of Ernest Hemingway. He spent most of the summer reading, and encouraging me to read, Hemingway's *Green Hills of Africa*. This was surely not one of Hemingway's best books, but it was an introduction to a style of writing I came to appreciate. I suspect George was attracted to the book more for the gruesome hunting depictions than for its literary value, but he studied it religiously.

George was the first atheist I ever knew. We spent hours debating religious issues, and I was amazed at his insights and the rationale for his position. Our debates helped strengthen some of my beliefs, but they also shattered some of my naive notions about religion. In retrospect, I think he saw religion in light of the way religious people treated him. People have to believe in the messenger before they will believe the message. One way or another, we are all messengers.

APRIL 16, 2006

At first glance, one might say it was a tree house or a platform for watching birds. That just goes to show you how deceptive things can sometimes be. The truth of the matter is that what we have here is a sailing ship commissioned in the spring of 2006 as the "Texas Ranger Pirate Ship." Those familiar with these kinds of things would know that the joint of PVC sewer pipe extending from its bow is in fact a cannon that never runs out of cannonballs. The ship has sailed each of the seven seas, where tumultuous battles have occurred with pirates who prey on defenseless vessels and villages. Sometimes the Texas Ranger Pirate Ship has fought alone against overwhelmingly sinister forces, but on occasion the ship has been supported by an armada of Eskimos. Treasure in the millions, recovered from battles on the high seas, has been distributed to poor people around the world.

Grandson Christian serves as the ship's captain, and his intrepid leadership has saved the ship from impending disaster on numerous occasions. His brother Thomas serves as first mate unless he is distracted by caterpillars, but even on his less focused days, he is an excellent officer.

Mariah, who joins the crew on some weekends, was offered the role of the kidnapped princess saved by brave men. She categorically rejected this offer, and demanded that she be allowed to serve as a swashbuckler like everyone else. Nothing could have pleased her Opa more. Some claim princess status because of their arrival via a royal birth canal, and other pretenders seek the title through lipstick, glitz, and perpetual smiles. An authentic princess, a princess of merit, is known for her inner qualities that radiate goodness, compassion, humility, and love. They do not seek the title, but it is one that they are awarded.

I serve the Texas Ranger Pirate Ship as Opa, lookout and chronicler of events. My service has taken me back in time and caused me to remember that, in the mind of a child, all things are possible. Sometimes in life what we choose to see may make all the difference.

MAY 5, 2006

On our walk today Chris identified the tracks of five different wildlife species. Thomas is a pretty good tracker as well, although he tends to specialize in trailing dung beetles. Nature is a great teacher we must listen to and obey.

MAY 26, 2006

There are so many endings now. The grains of sand in the hourglass fall freely and pelt my body. It is as though I am in a free fall into helplessness, for each new day shows me I am less, physically, than I was the day before. Somewhere in the heart of darkness, depression lurks and wants to control me. He wants my sunsets, my dinner-table conversations, my view of the mountain, my time with old friends, and especially my nights.

Sometimes I feel like giving him what he wants, but I know if I do I will be submitting to this disease. I won't give in, at least not as long as I can think straight.

In seminars on crisis management, I always talked about the importance of ignoring the things you can do nothing about and concentrating on the things you still have control over. When I think about it, there are things that I can still control. I can still walk. I can still write on my computer by using a voice-activated program. I can still talk. I have difficulty turning pages, but I can still read. Though ever so weakly, I can still touch her with my right hand. I can still direct the operations on this ranch. No good thing ever comes from concentrating on weaknesses; I must build my future around those things I can still control.

JUNE 2, 2006

A Houston jury this week found Enron executives Ken Lay and Jeff Skilling guilty on numerous charges of fraud and conspiracy. In an earlier time, these two men headed the world's largest energy company and were seen as unstoppable in their march to make it the most powerful company in the world. But then something went terribly wrong.

As the world was to learn, they were not leaders, they were plunderers. Through various fraudulent accounting practices and deceptive reports to stockholders, they, and others in the company like them, looted company assets. In their wake, twenty-one thousand Enron employees lost their pensions and the price of Enron stock plummeted. Unapologetic to the end and still maintaining their innocence, both vowed to appeal the jury's decision.

Both Lay and Skilling are examples of the blind arrogance that often possesses those at the top. They surround themselves with people who tell them what they want to hear. They are insulated from the ground level, the real people who make the company work, and they soon begin to believe the myths of their own press clippings. In this type of climate, the fortunes of an organization are influenced more by charismatic personalities than by sound management practices. Those who promote their own well-being, imperial images, and popularity at the expense of integrity-driven leadership inevitably have their day of reckoning.

One person who saw through the Enron facade was vice president Sherron Watkins. She warned Lay in August of 2001 that the company was on a perilous course, but she was ignored. In reflecting back on her time at Enron, she had this to say about Enron's corporate leadership:

> By taking care of himself, Lay violated one of Jesus' leadership lessons, found in Mark 9:35: "if anyone desires to be first, he must be the last of all and servant of all." We

need to applaud the servant leader, the one who clearly distinguishes that the interest of the organization and its customers, employees and investors (in that order) come first, not his own. Humility is a critically important trait in leaders. We have to ask ourselves, "Is our society cultivating humanity?" Do we exhibit that trait individually and collectively as a nation? Will we stop and learn from the Enron lesson in leadership failures, or will we just shrug our shoulders and thank God we're not Ken Lay?[8]

I always looked forward to the beginning of an academic year when I had the opportunity to speak to the new freshman class. I welcomed them to campus and invited them to become a part of the legacy of our institution. During the course of our time together, I would also ask them to close their eyes and imagine what their life would be like twenty-five years into the future. Given the fact that the meeting took place at eight o'clock in the morning and that some of them had been recreating well into the morning hours, involving them in an exercise with their eyes closed was risky business. Fortunately, most of them came back into the land of the living when the exercise was over.

I never asked them to say what images they conjured up, but I did say I hoped their image of the future involved family and a prosperous life doing meaningful work. I went on to say that if their images of the future reflected no social consciousness or concern for the environment then, in my view, their lives would be less than what they could have been and that we had failed them as an educational institution.

What is the measure of a life lived well? I don't think I am smart enough to answer that question, but I do believe that Robert Greenleaf, the father of the servant leadership movement, spoke clearly on the matter when he talked about the effect leaders have on the lives of others:

Do those served grow as persons; do they, while being served, become healthier, wiser, freer, more autonomous, more likely themselves to become servants? And what is the effect on the least privileged in society; will they benefit, or at least, will they not be further deprived?[9]

Entertainer June Carter Cash, in talking about her life said, "I just want to *matter*."[10] This simple, yet so powerful, message speaks volumes to leaders. People who matter in our lives are enablers, healers, and givers. Those who live lives well matter to a lot of people. Ken Lay and Jeff Skilling could have mattered to a great number of people, but they made other choices.

JUNE 5, 2006

From our back porch on a clear day you can see across the valley of the Llano River to Mason Mountain some fifteen miles away. A small knoll just this side of Mason Mountain is the place where some of the George Todd family were massacred in early January of 1865.

George Todd was a Virginia aristocrat who came with the first settlers to Mason County. A lawyer by profession, he served as the first county clerk and later became a prominent businessman. He settled on land south of Mason, next to his wealthy father-in-law, Joshua Peters. On a bitter cold morning, along with his wife, Dizenia, their attractive thirteen-year-old daughter, Alice, and a young black female slave whose name has been lost, he ventured forth for a ride into the town of Mason. Alice Todd was riding behind her father, while the servant girl rode behind Mrs. Todd.

When they approached the knoll now known as Todd Mountain, they noticed a group of mounted horsemen coming toward them. At first they surmised that the group were cowboys tending their stock. As the group drew closer, though, they could see the faces of marauding Indians. The Todd party immediately tried to outrun their pursuers, but to no avail. The servant girl was shot and killed, and Mrs. Todd, impaled by an arrow, slipped from her saddle. When the attack began, George Todd's horse shied and then broke into a dead run. In the commotion, young Alice fell to the ground. While she screamed for her father to stop, she was seized by her pursuers. George Todd, who later maintained he could not stop his runaway horse, left his family behind.[11]

He rode his horse into Mason some four miles away, where the townsmen immediately assembled and raced to the scene of the assault. They found Mrs. Todd near the fatally wounded slave girl, still alive, though barely. There were reports that one of her assailants stopped briefly to comfort her, murmuring aloud, "poor squaw, poor squaw." She would survive five more agonizing days, riddled by both physical and mental pain. Alice Todd had been taken captive by the attackers. The Indians, who were either Kiowas or Comanches, took their captive and began a horrendous ride back toward the sanctuary of the Great Plains. They were pursued by several groups of citizens, but falling snow dramatically slowed the searchers' pace. Once on the Great Plains, the Indians separated into three different groups, rendering further pursuit all but impossible.[12]

Alice Todd's stepbrother, Jim Smith, was in Arkansas serving the Confederacy when he heard what had happened to his family. He immediately asked for, and was granted, a furlough. When he reached his home, he vowed to spend the remainder of his life searching for his sister. In the following years, he traveled throughout the Southwest following one reported sighting after another, hoping to find his sister. There were numerous reports, some as far away as Kansas, of the girl living among various tribes. Some say she married, had a child, and refused to leave her adopted people. Another report claimed that she froze to death in the first days following her capture. Whatever the case, she was never seen by her family again. Jim Smith never gave up hope of finding his sister. He died an untimely death when he fell from a bluff to the Llano River.[13]

Mrs. Todd is buried alongside the servant girl in a quiet country cemetery at the base of Todd Mountain. George Todd went on with another life. Whether his story about the runaway horse was true or not, there were enough skeptics who believed he had abandoned his family to make his life miserable. He knew what happened that January day, his wife knew what happened, and Alice Todd knew what happened. That burden, however light or heavy, remained with him for the rest of his days.

A lot of people think Alan Le May's acclaimed novel *The Searchers*, which later became a movie classic, was loosely based on the events at Todd Mountain. My friend and historian, Scott Zesch, takes issue with this view, but there is a striking parallel between fact and fiction here.

Most days when I am outside, I make a point to look across the Llano Valley toward Todd Mountain. Like so many places in the Hill Country, it speaks to me of the human drama that unfolded here long ago. It also reminds me that in varying degrees, we all have to make "Todd Mountain decisions." There can be no rehearsal for these moments, but we do have choices as to where our moral compass will point us.

Chapter 5
The Leader as Critical Thinker

The reasonable man adapts himself to the world; the unreasonable one persists in trying to adapt the world to himself. Therefore, all progress depends on the unreasonable man.
—George Bernard Shaw[1]

John Wayne did not make many critically acclaimed movies, but *The Searchers*, produced in 1957 and directed by John Ford, ranks as an American classic. Even today the movie has a cult following among some scholars of Western history and popular culture enthusiasts.

In leadership seminars I have used one segment of the movie as an example of how leaders sometimes think in perilous circumstances. In the movie, John Wayne comes home to Texas from the Civil War, bitter over the war's outcome and angered by the fact that the woman he loves has married his brother. His arrival at his brother's home immediately creates tension, for it is obvious that the two people who really love each other are not the husband and wife. Early on the morning following his return, a company of Texas Rangers comes to the ranch seeking recruits to pursue a band of cattle rustlers. John Wayne agrees to join the Rangers, but he insists that his brother remain home in case the real cattle thieves are not rustlers, but Comanches seeking to draw the ranchers away so their homes and families will be vulnerable to attack. At this point the chase begins and the posse rides away looking for battle.

After a long pursuit the men find one of the missing cattle. To their horror, the animal has been killed by a Comanche lance. They now realize that, from the start, this has been a murder raid designed to lure them away from their homes. The behavior of the men now becomes an interesting point of study. For the most part, a general panic breaks out among the group.

Some men scream the names of their loved ones and one begins to cry. Amid the pandemonium, most of the men frantically turn their horses and race to the aid of their beleaguered families.

Unlike the others, John Wayne dismounts and begins to remove the saddle from his horse. His nephew frantically cries out to him, "Are you coming or aren't you?" John Wayne reminds him that the horses have traveled forty miles and that they need grain and rest. The young man looks at his uncle as if he is crazy, and then turns away and rides into the dust. In the next scene, John Wayne races across the plains past his nephew, who is carrying the saddle from his dead horse. His nephew yells for him to stop, but Wayne, astride a rested horse, rides on.[2]

Reactive versus Responsive Behavior

Two kinds of behavior were exhibited among the rescuers. Most of them quickly fell into a reactive-behavior mode—meaning there was an emergency, it was time-sensitive, and they immediately reacted to it. Reactive behavior is most often provoked by pain and/or emotions in our lives. This kind of thinking evolves from our most primitive, "reptilian" brain, whose primary function is to ensure our survival. When reactive behavior sets in, we don't give much thought to consequences; we just want to fix the problem or relieve the pain as soon as possible. The nephew and most of the searchers were exhibiting reactive behavior when, without much forethought, they rushed off to the aid of their loved ones.

Response thinking, on the other hand, results in decisive behavior based on reason. Among the searchers, only the character played by Wayne rose above the emotional frenzy to think responsively. He immediately foresaw the consequences of another forced march. He had the same goal as the other men, but he knew that he would be more likely to help his loved ones by resting his horse than by riding it to death on the prairie. Though he was obviously distraught, he responded to the issue with foresight and contemplation rather than by reacting to it emotionally.

Both reactive thinking and responsive thinking have their place in leadership, but when used inappropriately they can produce disastrous results. History is filled with episodes of both leadership successes and failures based on reactive and responsive thinking.

There are some situations in which reactive thinking is appropriate. For instance, if the leader of a ski patrol on a mountain slope observes an avalanche bearing down on the group, he or she needs to react as soon as possible. There is no time for discussion or contemplation. They need to move and to do it immediately. Most issues in life, however, do not have to be settled by reactive thinking. When reactive thinking is used in highly emotional situations, it often diminishes the chances for a desirable solution.

In 1875, an incident happened in our peaceful community that set in motion a reign of terror, pitting neighbor against neighbor. At that time the Texas frontier, and our county in particular, was plagued by cattle rustling. When five young men said to be involved in cattle thievery were jailed, some hotheads in the community demanded immediate justice. That night a mob stormed the jail and took the prisoners a short distance away where four of the five were hanged. The fifth prisoner, who owed his life to a malfunctioning hangman's knot, raced into the darkness and was never seen in the county again.[3]

The reactive behavior of those who organized the mob did nothing to bring justice to the county. The primary effect of their action was to start the Mason County War, which, over the next year, made the little community of Mason the murder capital of Texas.

What Makes a Responsive Leader?

Leaders who lead well in difficult circumstances rise above the emotional climate. These responsive leaders may be described in various ways, but I believe responsive leaders are ultimately known by the way they process three questions in crisis situations.

Question 1: What's the Basis of the Problem?

Some leaders try to fix the situation, not the problem. This occurs when the leader thinks reactively and thus tries to apply a superficial Band-Aid to internal hemorrhaging within the organization. For instance, high absenteeism in any organization may not be so much an employee health problem as it is a morale problem among people who get little or no fulfillment from their work. Once it infects an organization, chronic absenteeism is seldom affected by management reprisals or, for that matter, employee incentive programs. Responsive leaders know to focus on improving the organization's health by creating an environment where employees feel they are doing meaningful work that is appreciated by others.

We parents often respond in superficial ways when we placate a child's temper tantrum in order to make the noise go away. Absence of pain, in this case cessation of screaming, does not mean the problem has been fixed. It merely means we are treating the symptom, not the problem. We can't fix the problem unless we come to terms with the broader context that the child does not understand limits and that there are consequences—not rewards—for temper tantrums.

Leaders who are adept in answering the question "What's the basis of the problem?" are usually *systems thinkers*.[4] They think beyond the simple situation to the complex whole, where systems that control our environment and our behavior originate.

For instance, those involved in agriculture have traditionally used synthetic fertilizers to increase crop and pasture production, with the theory being that synthetic fertilizer provides nutrients that plants need to grow; when they are applied correctly, production increases. Some scientists now point out that, over time, the chemicals in synthetic fertilizers actually destroy life-supporting microbes in the soil.[5] When this occurs, more fertilizer is needed over the years to produce the same amount of forage.[6] In other words, an inverse relationship has been created where the more synthetic fertilizer you apply, the less you produce.

Systems thinkers tell us that a more desirable approach would be to strengthen the systems that naturally sustain plant growth. For instance, nature's systems are strengthened by the introduction of organic materials, rotational grazing, and controlled burning. As the microbial activity in the soil becomes healthier, a sustainable environment can develop.

In his own way the legendary chief Seattle of the Native American Duwamish tribe was a systems thinker long before anyone coined the term:

> What befalls the earth befalls all the sons of the earth. This we know: the earth does not belong to man, man belongs to the earth. All things are connected like the blood that unites us all. Man does not weave this web of life. He is merely a strand of it. Whatever he does to the web, he does to himself."[7]

From its inception, Southwest Airlines has done a masterful job in using systems thinking to promote positive employee relationships. In my interviews with Southwest employees, I have been repeatedly told how enjoyable it is to work in that organization. When pressed for specifics, employees talk about their opportunities to share in profits, the company's commitment to collegiality in the workplace, the mutual respect between management and employees, and the open communications and the fun they have at work.[8]

A carrot-and-stick operation does not produce these kinds of results. Given the competition in the industry, a small company like Southwest could never have succeeded without a different way of thinking about doing business. The company understood that no silver bullet can ensure organizational health. In their case, management at Southwest chose to focus on structures that provoke behaviors that *determine* events, rather than just reacting to events.[9] The multiple systems that affect the lives of employees became a primary concern for the company's leadership. When systems are headed in a direction beneficial to both employees and the company, good things are likely to happen.

Question 2: What Will Happen if I Do Nothing?

A fundamental law physicians are taught in medical school is "First, do no harm."[10] I see little evidence that this law is emphasized in MBA programs, but it should be. All natural systems want to stay in balance. The human body has immense healing powers that, when left to do their work, can often restore a diseased body to a healthy state. The ecological systems around us will balance themselves unless interfered with by humankind. Although more erratic in their healing responses, social systems also seek an equilibrium. Leaders who lead well understand that wounds to the body, the ecosystem, and social systems are all immediately addressed by healing agents within the system that seek a return to normalcy.

If natural consequences will cure a problem *without anyone being hurt*, leaders should consider just staying out of the way. This is particularly true for those who lead families. Parents who consistently intervene in their children's disputes with playmates and teachers are interfering with natural consequences. Their children quickly learn there are no consequences for irresponsible behavior if the parent will always make things right for them. In such cases, the parent is setting the stage for a troubled adulthood down the road. Natural consequences in the give-and-take world in which children have to live are among life's great lessons.[11]

As I think back on my time as a university department head, I now see that I made a mistake when I once chose to intervene in a certain situation that would have been better left alone. The case in point occurred when I sought to build a protective barrier around a promising new faculty member who I thought was being mistreated by colleagues. I assumed the problem was caused by professional jealousy, but I did not know about some of this professor's actions that had greatly antagonized colleagues. Later, when the truth began to unfold and the professor had left for another institution, a senior member of the staff told me in no uncertain terms that the faculty would have solved this problem on their own if I had left it alone. I think he was correct in his assessment. Artificial climates generally make things worse.

It is sometimes quite difficult for newly appointed leaders to resist the temptation to interfere with systems that are in place and working. They know they are expected to act like leaders, which for some people means making changes and asserting power. This is not to say that leaders should not be agents of change, but the caution is to "First, do no harm."

One time, a person told me about a recently appointed leader whose behavior could be predicted according to whatever new management book he had on his desk that month. Those who reported to this individual felt they had to suffer through endless change for the sake of change. In this case, the leader would have been wise to first seek to understand the systems in place and then base any changes thereafter on identified needs, rather than on the latest management fad.

Question 3: How Can I Best Respond to the Problem?

In the abundant literature on the subject, management gurus have given us any number of problem-solving models. I would suggest, however, that no decision-making model holds up in every circumstance because all decision making, in the end, is situational. Good problem solvers are more likely to be responsive leaders who understand the psychology of human behavior, who are grounded in what they think they should do to help people reach their potential, and who have the courage to make tough decisions.

Responsive Leaders Nurture Survivors

Leadership effectiveness is inevitably linked by others in the organization to the leader's ability to solve problems. Unfortunately, solutions are not always readily apparent and there will be some problems leaders cannot resolve. Sometimes the best thing leadership can do is to help others cope with a bad situation. For instance, physicians cannot say for sure that they have cured certain autoimmune diseases.[12] They can often eliminate symptoms and give patients a new lease on life for many years. For other patients, the best they can do is to make them comfortable and to help them cope psychologically with the ordeals the future will present.

This same scenario sometimes plays itself out for those who have to provide leadership in the wake of tragedies. Following tragedies such as school shootings, industrial accidents, transportation disasters, or a death in the family, nothing the leader can do will change what has happened. In these situations, the leader's role is to nurture survivors.

The life of acclaimed writer Kate Chopin offers one example of responsive leadership in the wake of tragedy. As a young woman in Louisiana in the late 1800s, she married into a prominent Creole family. Her husband was a wealthy plantation owner with inherited land and enormous stature in the community. As Oscar Chopin's wife, she soon learned that she had married not only a man but also a lifestyle. Among her planter circle of friends, women were supposed to be decorative, not utilitarian. Creole wives epitomized conspicuous consumption in that their jewelry, their servants, their clothes, and their pretentious homes were all reflections of the wealth of their husbands. Kate Chopin never fit easily into the life of privilege, but she bore her husband five children and did her best to create a happy home for her family.

Her idyllic world came crashing down on her when her husband died suddenly. She learned soon thereafter that her husband had mismanaged his inherited fortune and that she was on the verge of losing all that they owned. At that time and in her culture, women did not manage business affairs. The societal expectations were for her to marry again, hopefully to someone who could resurrect the family fortune. Kate Chopin, however, was not like most people. She had no interest in marrying for the sake of economic security, nor did she want her five children to be a part of an unwanted blended family. She knew she could not bring her dead husband back to life nor could she immediately restore the family's wealth, but she did have a plan.

She decided to manage the plantation herself. She immediately immersed herself in every facet of the plantation's operation.

She hired an overseer to do the things she could not do, but through it all she provided leadership for the preservation of the plantation and for her family. In the course of one year, she was successful in making the plantation solvent. She also turned her life-long passion for writing into a successful career as she authored both short stories and several novels. Kate Chopin had the audacity to believe she could cope with what many felt was an irreparable situation. She not only coped, she thrived in that environment, the integrity of her family remained intact, and the literary world gained a new voice.[13]

Responsive Leaders Have the Courage to Make Unpopular Choices

Leaders who spend all their time worrying about personal consequences in decision making are going to lose their followers. This is not to say that leaders should be abrasive or condescending, but a primary function of leadership is to deal with controversy. Those who shrink from this task usually become leaders in name only.

In 1951 when General Douglas MacArthur overstepped his bounds, making policy statements about the war that ran counter to the president's, Truman relieved him of command. General MacArthur was easily one of the most popular generals in our country's history. His command of the Pacific Theater during World War II and his brilliant tactical maneuvers in Korea gained him renown. General MacArthur and many of his ardent supporters thought he was untouchable. In relieving MacArthur of his command, President Truman made one of the most controversial decisions in the history of the presidency.[14] As bitter as the personal costs were to him, President Truman had made the right decision, for he reaffirmed the principle of civilian rule in our government.

Once long ago, I was struggling with an administrative decision with no easy solution. Finally, I took my question to a senior administrator I respected. After looking at all the options, this person agreed that there was no quick fix to this problem, but he did pose a question: "How do you think you will feel about your decision twenty years from now?" With that thought in mind, there was only one option worth considering.

Responsive Leaders Seek to Minimize Executive Decision Making

Sometimes leaders project a "godfather" image to others in the organization. The message is simple: "Control is at the top; look to me for all good things, and I will take care of you." Godfathers create leader-dependent organizations staffed by people afraid to make decisions.

Contemporary views of the way armies are commanded in the field exemplify this point. The German army in World War II was as regimented as any fighting force ever to take the field of battle. Its rigid adherence to its strictly defined command structure sometimes worked against it.[15] For example, if a lieutenant was killed or disabled in battle, the platoon often remained leaderless until a new officer arrived at the scene. Such was not the case with the U.S. Army, where command could immediately be passed to the next ranking person within the platoon, who then assumed leadership of the troops if need be.

A primary function of leadership is to set employees free from an excessive dependence on leaders in order to get things done. The more autonomy employees have in making decisions, the greater the breadth of brainpower involved in running the organization.[16]

In the future, the fate of families, countries, and this planet will be determined by our acceptance or rejection of responsive leaders who have the ability to look beyond simplistic solutions to the complex, interconnected relationships that spawn systems that have the ability to protect or destroy us.

JUNE 7, 2006

One thing that bothers me about this disease is that it is linked to the New York Yankees. That is not to say I do not admire Lou Gehrig immensely. He was a tremendous baseball player and a fine gentleman. It is just that I never liked the New York Yankees. Most of the boys in our little town either liked them or hated them. They dominated the 1950s like no other team has ever dominated a sport, but my heroes were elsewhere. Whenever we could get out of work during the summer, we sat by the radio listening to Dizzy Dean and the baseball "Game of the Day." My greatest hope on those days was that I might hear a broadcast of a Yankees-Red Sox game, or in other words, a game between the Yankees and Ted Williams.

Many people have said that Williams was the greatest pure hitter of all time. I suspect that could be true, but comparing one generation's legends to those of another is hardly an exact science. However, when you look back from our time to the era in which he played, he was the last player to have a batting average above .400; he won the Triple Crown three times; he led the league in home runs four times; he led the league in batting average six times; and he was the oldest player (40) in league history to win a batting title. He did all this and more despite the fact that opposing pitchers seldom had to worry about a Babe Ruth, a Mickey Mantle, or a Willie Mays following him in the batting order. He was the all-time leader in on-base percentage (.481) largely because opposing pitchers would rather walk him than pitch to him.[17]

What impressed me the most about Williams, and why I think he belongs in a class by himself, was the way he approached the game. He loved to play baseball and he was a tremendous competitor, but I think he played more against a *standard* than he did against other players. He admitted he wanted to be the best hitter who ever played the game, but he repeatedly jeopardized his chances for that legacy by choices he made.

As the 1941 season began to wind down, Williams was on track to become the first player since Bill Terry to finish the year batting above .400. On the last day of the season, when Boston was scheduled for a doubleheader, Williams was hitting .3996, which, when rounded off, would have given him the coveted .400 average for the season. His manager encouraged him to sit out the doubleheader and not risk having a bad day. Williams would have no part of any capitulation. He was not that kind of player. He played in both games, got six hits in eight attempts, and finished the season with a .406 average.[18]

He should have been named most valuable player more than twice. Three times he won the Triple Crown (hits, home runs, and stolen bases) only to see the MVP designation go to another player. Many attribute this to the fact that Williams was a high-strung, private person who refused to cater to sports-writers. His contempt for them was legendary, and he paid a price for it.

A story often told about Williams involves his negotiating a new contract with the Red Sox. Following a mediocre year for him, he met with the front office, where he was told they planned to offer him a modest pay raise. Williams immediately rejected the offer. He emphatically told management the contract offer was not acceptable because his play the year before did not merit a salary increase. Amazingly, Williams went on to suggest that based on his performance, he actually deserved a salary reduc-tion. I cannot imagine that happening in these times.[19]

The most memorable day in his career, I believe, was his last game. Though it was not the last game of the 1962 season, it was Boston's last home game that year. When Williams came to bat in the eighth inning, many of the fans realized they might be seeing the old warrior batting for the last time. He walked to the batter's box amid a thunderous ovation from the fans. In his usual fash-ion, he ignored the ovation and concentrated on Baltimore Orioles pitcher Jack Fisher. On the third pitch, Fisher delivered, and Williams hit a towering home run over the center-field fence. Just as he had done 521 times before, Williams, head down, cir-cled the bases and walked to the dugout, oblivious to the pande-monium around him. Despite another prolonged ovation and encouragement by players and management to come out and tip his hat to the crowd, Williams remained in the dugout. It was not the Williams way to do so; he played against a standard. Williams picked that moment to retire, and he never played in another game.

Today I sometimes think about Ted Williams when I see exhibitionists grandstanding after they make a good play. I find it painful when I see great athletes, past their prime, humiliate themselves in games just to keep the paychecks coming. How you leave something is every bit as important as how you entered, and when you are not playing against a standard, it is easy to lose sight of what really matters.

I wonder what would happen in the next presidential election if one of the two major parties would nominate a person committed to a set of standards, rather than one committed to satisfying the demands of those who profit from politics. Most political analysts say it would be all but impossible to elect a person like that to the presidency. That is the same thing they said in the 1860 presidential election when the Republican Party nominated a backwoods country lawyer from Illinois.

Ted Williams had a great deal to do with my retiring at age 58. I never told anyone that because I did not want to imply that I had hit a home run as a college president. Things were going well at the college: a major building program had just been completed, we had increased our reserves, the college's rapport with alumni was excellent, and institutional effectiveness indicators were strong. There were probably any number of people who could have led the college better than me, but I knew for sure I had done all I could do for the institution. I also knew that for the first time in my professional life, I was tired. I could have stayed on for another five to ten years and been much better off financially, but for me there was only one pace I could ever run.

Coasting into my last at-bat was not a satisfactory option.

June 18, 2006

Today is Father's Day. Two good men call me Dad, and I am immensely proud of both of them. My pride in them is based on many things, not the least of which is the fact that both of them are giving their lives to public service. Jeff spends his days trying to keep people from harming our country, and Chad spends his days trying to protect our wildlife and our environment. Both could have pursued other, more lucrative endeavors, but their sense of service prevailed. Our family has been so blessed by them.

A special treat on this Father's Day for both Veleda and me was the news that we will be grandparents again. Jeff and Jennifer will have a new arrival in January.

JUNE 19, 2006

Mariah is spending this week with us and she is marvelous company. Like Christian and Thomas, she sees everything around her with a sense of wonder most of the world has forgotten. We spent a long time on the porch swing yesterday afternoon talking, and I taught her to sing "Dixie." While we were swinging, she asked me why my arms don't work anymore. I told her that sometimes when people get older they start to lose some of their strength. She then asked me, "Opa, are you going to die soon?" I told her only God knew the answer to that question.

JUNE 20, 2006

In Lubbock, Texas, if you look far enough you can see the back of your head.—Joe Ely[20]

This time of the year is hotter than the devil in the Texas Hill Country. Once the sun begins to set, however, the temperature drops quickly and the magic of the hills takes your mind away from the day. That special moment, when the sun is burning itself out, enchants romantics and photographers alike, and it should be shared with kindred spirits. Our friends Dennis and Kay Evans own a beautiful home near the Llano River. Dennis has connections to the Austin music scene, and during the summer months he invites singers and songwriters up for live performances. At sunset, neighbors and friends, lawn chairs in hand, circle around the patio behind their century-old home. There we sip wine and hear a refreshing blend of Americana free of glitz but touched by the spirits.

Last Saturday Jeff, Jennifer, Chad, and I joined a number of others gathered to hear Texas legend Joe Ely. For the better part of three hours we sat there totally engrossed in this man's songs and his guitar and harmonica music. He wrote most of the songs he sang, and the depth of feeling in his work reminded me that when he looks at people, sunsets, highways, and open spaces, he sees things others cannot see. Over the years he has opened performances for the likes of Bruce Springsteen, the Rolling Stones, Paul McCartney, and Linda Ronstadt. He belongs to a unique breed of Texas singer-songwriters such as Jimmy Dale Gilmore, Guy Clark, Butch Hancock, and Lloyd Maines, whose acoustical sounds have brought them wide acclaim in the United States and Europe—but not necessarily riches. Those privileged to sit in on late-night jam sessions with him and his friends never forget the experience.

I could not help but compare him to some of the Nashville crowd today who prance around the stage in tight jeans and under cowboy hats that have never been in the sun. These entertainers have been anointed by the Nashville kingmakers who package them and sell them to the public. Their songs, written by someone else, all sound alike, and if you listen closely, you will hear that they don't have much to say.

Joe Ely might have made it in Nashville had he tried. He certainly is good enough, but performers like him usually have their own set of values. My sense is that he is more dedicated to an art form than what the kingmakers would have him be. If this were not true, he wouldn't write the kind of songs he does. Joe Ely has been described as a songwriter more interested in writing songs that will please his friends than the world.

He told us that the next day he was driving to California. It is possible that somewhere along Interstate 10, Joe Ely will pass an expensive, eastbound, customized bus. Inside will be a New Age country star headed back to the riches of Nashville, but the truth is that the real talent is headed west.

June 30, 2006

If it were not for death, there could not be life. We sometimes see death as an unnatural event when, in fact, it is the most natural of events. Flowers bloom, have their moment of glory, and then pass on to become nutrients for the next spring. We are all flowers, in that life gives us the opportunity to nurture the coming spring.

This is not to say we should not seek to live well and long. It is to say that the moment we accept nature's cycle, the more likely we are to enjoy the time we have and to do something worthwhile in our lives.

JULY 1, 2006

New Orleans soul singer Irma Thomas was interviewed on National Public Radio today. As with so many New Orleans residents, Hurricane Katrina did significant damage to her home and property. When asked about the storm's aftermath and the controversial government responses to the disaster, she said, "I am too blessed to be depressed."[21] The dragon was knocking, but she wouldn't let him in.

Chapter 6
Are We Living Life Deeply Enough?

Are we living life deeply enough? I think probably not. Too often, we sail our life's course on a sea six thousand miles wide and six inches deep. Along the way, we tend to gobble up rather than savor life's blessings. Far too many Americans live life on the weekends and holidays, and tolerate some kind of existence in between. Somewhere along the way, we are missing something.

A report on the CBS news this morning explored the level of happiness among people in various nations. The United States ranked fifteenth—well behind several nations we often describe as underprivileged. Given the number of people in our country today who are involved in the abusive use of controlled substances, who are addicted to therapy, and who cannot build meaningful relationships, it seems many of us may just scratch at the surface of life. Whatever our troubles, the depth of life we seek often eludes us because the choices we make force us back to the surface.

Electronic Media Drown Out the World around Us

It is easy today to permit television and other electronic devices to come between us and a deeper life. This is not to say there is anything inherently wrong with television. At times there are some exceptionally good educational programs and TV events that compel our attention. I would also never go so far as to say that we should not watch baseball games. In general, however, the medium is intellectually and spiritually sterile. We permit it to take from us critical time we can never recover.

Nowhere is this blight more telling than in what television does to family interactions. Time-honored family conversations after dinner are giving way to a rush to watch who Donald Trump will fire tonight or what new person on *Survivor* will be stabbed in the back. Surely there is more to life than this. We allow this intrusion even though psychologists have been telling us for years that families who take the time to dine together in the evening are much more likely to remain intact through the years.

At the end of World War II, we lived with my grandparents for several months. Grandpa and Grandma Taylor were share-croppers who lived in an unpainted house without electricity or indoor plumbing. My uncles Tom and Zeke, who had recently returned from the war in the Pacific, also lived with us. The adults of the family labored in the fields from daybreak until dark. My grandmother's day began before dawn when she put biscuits in the wood cookstove and ended in the darkness of night when she threw her dishwater over the backyard fence, and she worked in the fields alongside everyone else. In her life-time she gave birth to ten children and, despite her many years of work in the fields, she was healthy well into her eighties.

By today's standards, one might think that the environment we shared was quite staid and void of excitement, but that was not the case. I lived for the after-supper conversations that took place around our supper table by the light of a kerosene lantern. There my uncles shared their tales of the South Pacific. Like most of the men of their time, they didn't talk much about the horrors of conflict. What they did talk about was ships, jungles, Hawaii, indigenous people, whales, comrades-in-arms, and all kinds of adventures that fascinated a six-year-old boy.

When my uncles were not carrying the conversation, my grandfather, who was a masterful humorist and storyteller, would enliven the evening with a yarn or two. He knew stories of his father, who had actually fought on both sides during the Civil War. Sometimes he would tell us some aspect of the gun battle in which his father shot and killed John Wolf on the Burnet County square in 1892. But mostly, I remember his humor, because he loved to tell funny stories. Whenever he went to town to sell butter and eggs and to buy the few grocery items not raised on the farm, I knew that night there would be stories from town that he would share with us.

Sometimes, fearing that the conversation that night might not get started right away on the subject I preferred, I would formulate leading questions beforehand. I got pretty good at asking Uncle Tom or Uncle Zeke questions that begged an answer. It was also relatively easy to get Grandpa going on a yarn, provided he was not too tired. I will always believe I received a priceless education around that table that could have occurred in no other way.

Later, when our sons were born, Veleda and I tried to maintain the tradition of after-supper conversation without distractions. I say "without distractions," yet there were times when I sat at the table but my mind was back at the office. At that time, however, we talked about what was happening in school and how the pets (dogs, cats, raccoons, gerbils, and horses) were doing, and we shared family generational stories. We celebrated in some conversations and we grieved in others. I realized something was going right when I once asked Jeff about one of his adventures, and he told me he would tell me about it later, when we were all at supper. I am convinced the time we shared strengthened our family and gave us something more than a superficial view of the depths.

Holding on to the Child within Us

There is a child within us who lives for a period of time but usually succumbs to adulthood. The adults I know who seem to be the most happy are those who have managed to stay in touch with the child within them, those who still believe in possibilities, hope, and fun.

At the conclusion of a presentation I once made to a group of professionals, called "Nurturing Others in the Organization," a person shared an interesting anecdote with me. She related how she previously worked for a nationally known social service agency that treated people with a variety of depressive disorders. During her tenure, she worked with people from numerous stations in life. One question she always asked any client was, "Tell me some things you are happy about." Children, she said, could always answer that question faster than any other group. Strangely, she said welfare mothers could always find something that they were happy about. The group who took the longest time to post a reply to her question—and sometimes went begging for an answer—consisted of successful male executives. If we let it, the child within us always looks for reasons to be happy.

Two weeks ago, we attended Mariah's dance recital. The program began when a chorus line of twelve four-year-old girls, clad in tutus, performed onstage. From their demeanor and the broad smiles on their faces, one could easily see these young ladies were happy to be performing. As might have been predicted, their performance was followed by wild applause from enthusiastic parents and kin. The smiles on their faces attested to their joy in dancing. In all fairness to the chorus line, I think it would be accurate to say that they performed a synchronized routine twelve different ways. In the minds of the performers, however, Carnegie Hall was just around the corner. As I watched Mariah and the others having so much fun, it was obvious that the occasional mistakes they made were of no consequence to them. I wondered, at the time, how long it would take the world to teach them about mistakes. Inhibitions due to fear of failure form the first stage of the metamorphosis that takes the child within from us.

Someone once said of the British that they are perpetually dedicated to being enthused about nothing. Those of us lucky enough to hold on to the child within never lose our sense of wonder. I continue to be amazed at the depths of joy Chris, Mariah, and Thomas find in the simplest things. Pretentious people who continually posture for the sake of others are just going to miss out on a lot of joy. Children find adventure in the most mundane of places. Commonplace things around them, like twigs and sticks, are really magic wands, and the animals they know have human qualities. Walter Cronkite, reporting to the world as astronaut Neil Armstrong stepped onto the moon, could not hide his sense of wonder, for his most memorable remark about the moment was "Wow!" If we let it, the child within will find a world of wonder.

There were times during my life when I let the child within get away from me. Whenever that happened, I or someone around me suffered. One case in point occurred when, at age thirty-six, I went back to graduate school full time. We took on this challenge even though I had some serious reservations about my scholastic ability to complete a doctorate. Over the next two years, I retreated into myself and pored over my studies with every ounce of zeal I had in me. When asked to coach Chad's Little League baseball team, I didn't have the time. When we should have been fishing, I was studying. There was no child in me then, and I regret now that I cannot get that time back.

Disconnecting from Significant People in Our Past

Our mobile society presents opportunities for us to develop acquaintances with a number of people. Once, during a night when I was having trouble sleeping, I started adding up the number of people who work in education whom I could call by name. I was amazed at the number of people I knew, and actually went to sleep before I finished the list. That doesn't mean, though, that our relationships were close.

Most people don't have deep relationships with a large number of people, but those we do have are critical to our well-being. Maintaining those relationships over time is no small task because the complexity of our lives too often encourages isolation.

A few years ago, I decided to try to reclaim our past together by contacting some individuals who had inspired me or who, over the years, had been trusted friends during both difficult and wonderful times. Several of the teachers on my list had passed away, but I was able to contact my high school track coach and my major professor in college. Beyond them, I was able to reestablish relationships with people going back to the time I was in the second grade.

The time and energy I spent on the search produced monumental rewards for me and I hope was beneficial to those I contacted. I feel particularly good about the experience, because the "call from the past" was not to ask for anything; rather, it was an invitation to share our lives together again. As I write this, several of those I contacted are helping me deal with the "dark cloud."

Working to Renew Our Lives

The veil that clouds your eyes shall be lifted by the hands that wove it.—Kahlil Gibran[1]

I used to say during my seminars that "Leadership is the art of living without an eraser." This adage not only applies to leadership; it is a reflection on life. Try as we might, there is nothing we can do about the mistakes of the past. The good news is that if we set our minds to it, we can still write the final chapters in the book.

The intellectual decay of some people begins while they are teenagers, and for others, learning is a lifelong experience. Just as some people squander family inheritances, others let intellectual gifts atrophy away. Unfortunately, when this happens, the individuals involved are then controlled by the circumstances around them, and their options in life are considerably limited.

I believe those who really explore the depths of life are in a constant state of self-renewal. They continue to grow spiritually and intellectually. Self-renewal has very little to do with intellect, but it has a great deal to do with the curiosity that can lead to greater fulfillment in life. The biographies of those said to have lived rich and productive lives, such as Winston Churchill, John Adams, Elizabeth Browning, and Thomas Jefferson, were marked by a perpetual quest for new learning opportunities.

Texas naturalist Roy Bedichek once related a most interesting tale about an incredible zest for learning that would not die. One day he was asked to go to the home of a University of Texas professor who had suffered a debilitating stroke. The man lived a distance from town in the hills surrounding Austin. When

Bedichek arrived, he was ushered into a bedroom where the man lay, barely able to move or speak. After a few formalities Bedichek politely inquired as to why he had been summoned. The professor motioned for Bedichek to sit down and not to speak. The two of them sat there in silence, the only sounds coming through the open window in the bedroom. Eventually, they could hear the sound of a bird chirping outside the window. In that moment the professor feebly asked Bedichek, "What kind of bird is making that noise?" Bedichek identified the bird for him. The professor smiled and thanked Bedichek for coming. The mystery had been solved and a thirst for more knowledge quenched. What an incredible drive to learn, to find meaning in a life that outwardly offered so little.[2]

The great crippler of self-renewal is a rushed life that offers no opportunity for reflection. For many years I thought I had no time in my day for study and self-renewal. I was too much involved in a frantic assault on life to contemplate the meaning of what I was doing or, for that matter, where it was all going to end. I was just trying to stay afloat.

In 1995, after reading some of Robert Greenleaf's work on personal reflection, I made a life-altering decision. My usual routine at that time had been to begin work at the office by seven or seven-thirty each morning. On that day I told my secretary that from seven-thirty to eight o'clock in the morning, I would be in my office with the door shut. She was to interrupt me only if there was an emergency, but otherwise I was not to be disturbed. For fifteen or twenty minutes of that period, I read something of substance. With that amount of time you can generally read a journal article, a book chapter, or chapters from the Bible.

After I finished reading each day, I spent the remainder of the time in prayer and reflecting on what I needed to do to make life better for those who were depending on me. The experience gave me a better perspective on the remainder of the day, my life, and my work that was invaluable. I continue to follow the practice today, and if I miss a day, I feel the loss. As far as the college was concerned, I could never tell that it missed the president's reflection time. Maybe the president was not as important as he thought.

Listening with Our Eyes

A psychologist friend of mine once came home from a long day at work to be greeted by his enthusiastic young daughter. When he sat down in the living room, his daughter jumped onto his lap, anxious to tell him about her day. The father picked up the newspaper as his daughter began relating stories to him. He smiled, nodded as she talked, and started to read the paper. Moments later the young girl broke down in tears. When the father inquired as to what was wrong, she said, "You're not listening to me." The father replied, "Honey, I have heard everything you said." Then, with the tears really falling, she said to her father, "Yes, but you are not listening with your eyes."

In conveying important messages, how we look at people is as important as anything we can ever express in words. Long ago when we were attending a family reunion, I walked across the room to join Veleda, who was talking with one of my aunts. When I got there, my aunt said, "I could just see the love in Veleda's eyes as she watched you come across the room." My aunt did not have to tell me what I already knew, but I thought it most interesting that a third person could see what was going on between us. She still touches me with her eyes every day.

When we live deeply enough, the messages we send others we care about are loaded with feeling and expressions of love. In the midst of the chaos of the world, a lingering stare between two loving people can restore and uplift us. It says we still do not take each other for granted; there is something going on between us. I have seen this message transmitted between bride and groom and from one nursing-home patient to another.

Those who explore the depths of life do so not by chance, but by choice. The conscious stream of choices they make enriches their lives and the lives of those around them immensely.

JULY 21, 2006

This week George Bush vetoed the stem cell research bill and, along with it, hopes for the approximately 100 million people whose families might have benefited from the research. He is on the wrong side of history.

JULY 23, 2006

My first university teaching position was at a small institution in Arkansas and it was there I met Big Ruby. There were two Rubys who worked in our building. One Ruby, a professor, was known as Little Ruby, and Big Ruby cleaned our building. I need not go into why Big Ruby was given that title, but I will say she was a black single mother and grandmother with several children. Her husband had long since left her, taking with him the possibility that she would know anything other than poverty and hard work for the remainder of her life.

I do not recall all the names of the people I worked with in that institution, but Big Ruby was unforgettable. I first became aware of her presence in the building one day when her gospel singing, in the hallway as she was cleaning, began to compete with the sterling lecture I was delivering to drowsy students. Not long thereafter, I stopped to talk with her one day and a marvelous friendship was born.

I soon learned that regardless of how badly my day had begun, Big Ruby would brighten it up. She laughed often and loud. Her laughter seemed to blast down the building corridors like the sound of a jet plane on the tarmac and always brought a smile to my face. In time, I began to look her up each day because she was medicine everyone needed. There were times when I could tell she was struggling with her circumstance, and in particular, the series of junk cars she drove to work, but she seldom complained. Her health was not good and there were concerns about her high blood pressure. Through it all she steadfastly refused to become a victim of her past. She saw each day as a gift from God and felt it was wrong to waste it on self-imposed misery.

On university campuses the one thing more predictable than interdepartmental bickering is the presence of some enormous egos. This is particularly obvious in the attention paid to rank and titles. New students and visitors often struggle with the protocol on whether to address teachers as doctor, professor, dean, etc. Big Ruby had no such problems; she simplified matters by calling everyone by his or her last name. From the day we met she referred to me as Boyd, and I doubt that she ever knew my first name.

Over the years I learned a great deal about life from Big Ruby. For one thing, she taught me that you do not have to be a licensed psychologist to analyze what people are thinking. She had an uncanny ability to read my mood long before I revealed it in words. In a politically correct environment, she saw through the superficiality of some who might champion her race. If you were not real, she could see it and she would tell you about it. Her first impressions of the new professors on campus proved to be pretty accurate in terms of their eventual success.

Four years after our arrival there, Veleda and I accepted an opportunity to return to Texas, and a long series of goodbyes ensued. In my heart I knew I wanted to do something to show Big Ruby how much I appreciated her, but I struggled with what would be appropriate. I could have given her a present of some kind, but what I really wanted to do was to affirm the value I placed on her friendship. I decided to ask her to go to lunch. I knew she would not go alone with me and because Veleda had a class during the noon hour, I asked another lady from the custodial staff to go along. Over lunch, Big Ruby quizzed me on why in the world we would want to move to Texas. (If you haven't heard, most Arkansans passionately believe that the worst view in the state is the one looking west from Texarkana.) After giving me a hard time she said, "You've got to do what you think is best." When we got back to the university parking lot, as if I were one of her children, she gave me a big hug and said, "Now Boyd, you take care of yourself." I never saw her again, but I still think about her.

JULY 29, 2006

Today for the first time, Christian saw me wearing the leg braces I must now use. He asked me what they were and I told him they would make my legs stronger. With the enthusiasm only he can muster, he said, "Opa, I am so happy you have the braces because now you will be able to run as fast as Tom and me." If we could all just hold on to our possibility thinking, how much better the world would be.

AUGUST 7, 2006

The curfew tolls the knell of parting day,
The lowing herd wind slowly o'er the lea,
The plowman homeward plods his weary way,
And leaves the world to darkness and to me.
—From "Elegy Written in a Country Churchyard"
by Thomas Gray[3]

In the 150-year history of our little fifty-six member Methodist church, the spiritual lives of many people have been shaped and a number of human dramas have unfolded. The church and the community around it were first known as Beaver Creek, but that good name was ruined by the U.S. Postal Service when it declared that "Beaver Creek, Texas" was too lengthy for a postal address. Legend has it that the name of the community was then changed to Hilda in honor of the local postmaster's girlfriend. At any rate, the name stuck and the Hilda United Methodist Church has carried on despite that handicap.

The church was formed in the days when the edge of the frontier lay to the east. Members of the congregation mostly came from the German settlements in Fredericksburg and New Braunfels established by the German Immigration Company. The church is located not far from the junction of the Llano River and Beaver Creek where Baron von Meusebach met with the Chief Katemoczy in 1847 to begin negotiating a peace treaty between the German settlers and the Comanches.

The peace treaty permitted settlement in the region, but in the early days, problems with Indians were common. Church birth records include the name of the legendary Indian captive Hermann Lehman, who was taken from his home in 1870. As an eleven-year-old boy, he was captured by Apaches and spent the next nine years as a member of that tribe, and later the Comanche tribe. In time he became the adopted son of the famous Comanche chief Quanah Parker. Although he was eventually returned to his family, he never really adjusted to life away from the

Indians. His exploits are well chronicled in the literature of the Southwest.

George Brandenberger, another church member, was shot from his horse in a running gun battle with Indians in 1876. He would most surely have been scalped if his mother, the day before, had not given him a short haircut. The Indian who shot him came to claim his scalp but deemed the shorn locks an unworthy prize and left him for dead. George walked home later that day.[4]

Some people predicted that the church could not survive modern times, given the mass migration to the cities and the fact that the nearest red light is thirty-five miles away. These failure forecasters did not understand the undaunted spirit of the parishioners. Our church, for the most part, operates as a pure democracy in that all members are invited to participate in administrative board meetings. I have to admit that sometimes, after two hours of furious debate over church maintenance issues, I have questioned the merits of democracy. In the end, however, the old adage "None of us is as smart as all of us"[5] prevails, and the church endures.

One experience I shall never forget came during church communion. It happened during the era of our first woman pastor, Sue Taylor, who came to our church directly from seminary. As a beginning pastor, she was particularly concerned with doing church rituals in a special way, and this was the case with communion. Her style was to stand in front of the congregation holding a freshly baked loaf of bread above her head and then tear it into two pieces to commemorate the breaking of the bread.

The loaves were furnished by members of the congregation, who often baked them at home. One Sunday morning the communion steward discovered, to her horror, that she had no bread for the service. Being miles from town, she quickly called her mother, who lived on a nearby ranch, detailing the current emergency. Her mother assured her not to worry because some hunters on their place had the day before given her a loaf of freshly baked bread. She would bring it to the service.

The church service went forward in the usual fashion and the time came to break the bread for communion. Attired in a flowing pastoral robe, the minister moved to the front of the communion table and picked up the loaf of bread. Then she lifted the loaf high above her head and solemnly tore it into halves. The reaction from the congregation was not immediate. Therefore, it was only when the pastor lowered the loaf that she discovered that, by breaking the bread, she had exposed one stick of sausage and another of cheese that had been baked into the bread. The steward who was sitting near the front of the church was the first to notice what happened. She and her family then broke into uncontrollable laughter. Pastor Sue never missed a lick; she calmly set the condiments on the communion table and went on as if nothing out of the ordinary had occurred.

Another memorable moment occurred last Sunday. The church service had not been going long when, from somewhere in the high-vaulted ceiling, a bat jumped out into space. By the time he had made two high-altitude flights around the sanctuary, the preacher had lost his audience. The erratic flight continued until the bat crashed into the wall and fell to the floor near the south entrance. At that point, Chad, the wildlife biologist, seized a cowboy hat from the hat rack and captured the intruder within. Feeling that the intruder was now immobilized on the floor under the hat, he went out to his car to get a pair of gloves for the more delicate task of removing it from the sanctuary.

At this point, the church settled down and began to focus on the children's handbell choir that was assembling at the altar. A false sense of security prevailed, however, for within minutes the bat escaped from his imprisonment and became airborne again. This time, accompanied by the children's handbell choir's rendition of "Holy, Holy, Holy," the bat began to perform a number of aerobatic stunts at a low altitude. Two quick swoops from the sky sent members of the back two rows into semiprone positions. Up he went again, darting forward in the sanctuary, this time dangerously close to the head of the choir director, who was oblivious to events transpiring behind him. The children's handbell choir, which had the best seat in the house for watching the acrobatics, was greatly amused, but with one eye on the director and the other on the bat, they laughingly continued to play.

Finally, the bat crashed into the wall behind the pulpit and fell to the floor again. By this time, the gloved wildlife biologist had returned to the scene. As he approached the pulpit area, he received congregational input in the form of pantomime as to where it was and what to do with it. Eventually he caught the culprit and carried him from the sanctuary while the congregation applauded.

On another occasion our church was to receive a visit from our district superintendent. Such visits are taken seriously by parishioners because the district superintendent appoints the pastors for all churches. On this day, the district superintendent was to preach on Sunday morning, and every effort had been made to make the church grounds and sanctuary as attractive as possible. When the district superintendent arrived, he changed into his doctoral robe and made his way toward the entrance of the church. I do not know how impressed he might have been with the appearance of the church and grounds, but I do know events at the door to the church got his attention. When he arrived there, one of our parishioners was in the latter stages of killing a rattlesnake that had coiled up within the doorway. I am not sure that he ever understood that this extraordinary happening for him was an ordinary event in our community.

Our church has its share of human drama, but there is also a profound spirituality in that place. In a world that seems to be changing at the speed of light, there is an incredible sense of permanency here. Other than renovations, most of the church buildings on the campus are the same as they were almost a century ago. The spring beneath the springhouse, which 125 years ago chilled the pastor's milk, continues to flow down the hillside. Nearby is the old smokehouse from whose rafters once hung smoked sausage, ham, bacon, and jerky. On any given day you can sit under one of the massive oaks surrounding the church and see white-tailed deer grazing in the churchyard. As they have done for countless seasons, each spring bluebonnets in the churchyard burst forth in an array of colors. During their season, they enrich the lives of all who pass by and then, like us, return to the dust from whence they came.

Most of the church's members are descendents of the founders of the church who are buried in the country cemetery at the foot of the hill. Whenever I see that place, I am reminded of Thomas Gray's poem "Elegy Written in a Country Churchyard," published in 1751. Those who wait for us at the foot of the hill once knew this place. From the bell tower of the church, you can see some of the homes that beckoned their weary return from the pastures and fields at the parting of each day. They lived, they loved, they laughed, and their legacy remains.

On Easter morning, parishioners and numerous visitors gather on the hill above the church to watch the sunrise. From where we sit, the sun rises opposite the church and briefly silhouettes the cross atop the steeple. In that fleeting moment, an incredible calmness settles onto the valley below; things are right with the world, and I am at peace.

SEPTEMBER 2, 2006

I have never held any person in high regard who could spell a word only one way.—Mark Twain[6]

After *Companions of the Blest* was published, I did some book signings and talks about the book around the state. At the signings, I did my part by fielding questions regarding what I thought about writing, and acted as though this was the kind of thing I did all the time. What those assembled did not realize was the irony of my talking with anyone about the King's English. I had barely passed my English courses in college, and I am to this day a terrible speller. For good reason, my English professors would never have predicted my publication of any work.

At the book signings, I was sometimes asked how people become successful writers. I could not answer this question, for there are too many exceptions to any rule I have ever seen. I do believe that those who write best write books that they would enjoy reading themselves. I am convinced there are some people who are born with remarkable talent who are destined to write. They may improve their style by study and by being around extraordinary teachers, but they come into the world with a remarkable gift possessed by very few. With a little luck and hard work, they may obtain critical acclaim, notoriety, and riches. These people, however, do not write all there is worth knowing.

There are others, not so talented, who might be able to write because they are extraordinary observers of human behavior. They see life as a series of unfolding adventures, and storytellers captivate them. If they live long enough, they eventually may have something to say. Though *Companions of the Blest* is a novel, there is very little in the book that I have not experienced or learned from people who told me treasured stories.

Therefore, I believe if we spent more of our time contemplating life rather than assaulting it, there can emerge a storyteller in each of us. People are never too old to begin to write, but they can wait too long to start collecting life stories. Most people have generational knowledge that needs to be passed to those who follow. Whatever our limitations may be in using the written word, whenever we write, we freeze a thought forever. Somewhere in time I suspect there will be people who will benefit from the stories we know.

SEPTEMBER 17, 2006

Dr. Roland Taylor, my maternal grandfather many generations removed, was burned at the stake on February 9, 1555.[7] In his time, he was a widely acclaimed intellectual and priest in the Anglican Church, as a doctor of both canon and civil law. By the accounts of those who studied his life, he was enormously popular with the parishioners he served in the village of Hadley, not far from London.

A student of the Reformation, he began his ministry when England was ruled by Edward VI and Protestantism was in favor. When Queen Mary, later known as Bloody Mary, came to the throne, the liberal ideas of the Reformation came into question, and persecution of those who did not pay homage to the Church in Rome began. It was inevitable that Roland Taylor would cross swords with the established church. He was a married priest with children, was loved by his parishioners, and he spoke against the corruption he saw in the Roman Catholic

Church. He was also in disfavor because he was the son of the Reverend John Taylor, one of the commissioners who ruled on the validity of the marriage of Mary's mother, Catherine of Aragon, to her father, Henry VIII.[8]

One morning Taylor arrived at his church to find the doors had been nailed shut. There he encountered papal authorities who accused him of crimes against the church and the queen. Unrepentant, he challenged their right to interfere with his ministry and was forcibly taken from his church. When word of his defiance reached London, his arrest was ordered. He was then transported to London and taken before Bishop Stephen Gardiner, lord chancellor of England, where he was accused of heresy.

When given the opportunity to speak during his hearing, Taylor said it was the bishop, not he, who was a heretic. He was immediately sent to prison, where he remained for two years. During that time he was told that if he would renounce his marriage and pledge to support the established church, he would be released. There were even implications he might be named a bishop if he agreed to return to the established church. When he rejected the overtures from the bishop, he was, in effect, announcing his own death sentence. Shortly thereafter the orders came that he was to be burned at the stake.

After his sentencing, he was given a brief opportunity to speak with Margaret, his wife. He embraced her tenderly and said that he loved her and the children. With his children and her welfare in mind, he also told Margaret it was his desire that she remarry. They embraced again, and she was taken away.

The execution was to take place not far from his home in Hadley. Probably fearing efforts would be made to free the prisoner, the sheriff of Essex and a contingent of armed men took him from the prison in the middle of the night. A hood was placed over the prisoner's head to keep him from being recognized by those they passed on the road.

On the two-day journey back to Hadley, the sheriff and most of his men were awed by Taylor's peaceful demeanor and loving treatment of his captors. Soon thereafter, the sheriff and others in the party began to plead with Taylor to save his life by recanting his vows. Taylor refused, for to do so would compromise a life's work and render his nine children illegitimate. When he humbly refused their request, the sheriff and others wept.

When they reached the place for his execution, a large crowd had gathered, along with his wife and some of his children. Taylor removed his outer garments and boots, and made gifts of them to those nearby. He was told he was not to speak and when he tried to do so, he was struck in the face by one of the guards.

Perhaps as a sign of respect for the priest, the villager whom the sheriff ordered to light the fire refused to do so. Finally, two bystanders threw lighted torches into the wood. As the flames began to rise beneath him, one of the guards struck Taylor in the head with a halberd (a flat ax), killing him instantly. He never knew the flames that consumed his body. Today an unhewn stone monument marks the place where Roland Taylor passed on to the next world.

Of all the blights on the history of humanity, religious intolerance may have left the worst mark. The 283 people martyred by Bloody Mary, and the thousands who lay dead in the wake of the Spanish Inquisition, are but a few of the multitudes who have fallen in the name of religion. The sword of intolerance casts a wide swath, and in this regard, neither Protestants, Catholics, Jews, nor Muslims can claim innocence from its vicious swing.

The same kind of madness that killed Roland Taylor in 1555 is at play in the world today. In Taylor's case, the evil force of intolerance wanted to obliterate all but its own kind, and the people who might have done something to save him did nothing. Then, as now, when we fail to oppose intolerance, we become a part of it.

All people of faith, including those in Muslim countries, should be stirred to action by what Islamic extremists are doing in the name of religion today. People of faith should be alarmed by fundamentalist Christians in the United States who believe that, of all the good people who have ever walked this planet, they alone have been selected to receive the true word of God. People of faith should realize that there are some religious zealots in Israel who will never be satisfied until all Muslims are dead or driven from the Holy Land. We cannot permit these people to control the world's agenda.

The problem can only be resolved when the world becomes outraged at intolerance and its consequences. An outraged world can sever the arteries that keep this malignancy alive. It is the role of moderates in all faiths to be a part of that outrage. Our approach should not stem from condescension, because our own checkered history offers us no license for piety. We should use our history, however, to remind our own people and the people of the world of the dire consequences that evolve from intolerance. We are Americans and, more than any other country, we have taught the world about tolerance. We need to speak the truth without fear, we need to do it now, and we need to do it on a global basis.

September 26, 2006

Malcolm Beck and his wife, Delphine, came by to visit today. They have just returned from a trip to South Africa where Malcolm was invited to speak to several agricultural groups. By any stretch of the imagination, Malcolm is one of the most interesting people I have known. Today he is a nationally acclaimed naturalist and his books are read by a worldwide audience.

His rise to prominence in his field, and the ownership of a hugely successful company, hardly parallel the typical success story. He was born during the Great Depression and spent his early years helping his farming family survive the droughts, low prices, and bankers. He did not attend college but chose instead to begin a career with the railroad, which lasted thirty-two years. Along the way he and Delphine purchased a hard-scrabble farm outside San Antonio. When he was not pulling a shift at the railroad, he spent his time trying to increase production on his worn-out farmland.

What happened after that had to do with Malcolm's insatiable curiosity and the fact that he is a systems thinker. He knew from his youth that organic materials plowed into farmland would increase production, but he did not understand why. Seeking answers, he talked with every agricultural authority who would give him some time, and he committed himself to read numerous journals typically reserved for PhDs. It was when he began a study of the natural processes that promote microbial activity in the soil that the mystery began to unfold. As University of Texas professors Drs. Dick and Pat Richardson would later help scientifically describe, Malcolm found that in healthy soils there is a "soil food web" composed of mutually dependent organisms.[9] These organisms thrive in an environment where organic matter exists in abundance. In creating healthy soils, they have an enormous influence on ecosystems, for "as these organisms eat, grow, and move through the soil, they make it possible to have clean air, clean water, healthy plants, and moderate water flow."

Next, Malcolm began using farm byproducts and other organic materials as compost, with significant results. By the time he retired from the railroad, he was making compost for himself, his neighbors, and in short order, an eager commercial market. Soon thereafter, he had a very successful business operation going, marketing a number of organically based agricultural products.

It goes without saying that using nature's way, and thereby avoiding the use of expensive and sometimes-toxic chemicals, threatens a major industry. Malcolm was soon to learn, however, that in a David and Goliath contest involving the Environmental Protection Agency, Goliath usually wins. The power that chemical companies have in using the Washington bureaucracy to keep competing products off the market is a national disgrace and should outrage all Americans. The industry's influence is not only confined to the nation's capital. Because they underwrite so many research projects, corporations have an inordinate amount of influence on what is, and is not, researched by universities. Malcolm continues to persist and, little by little, the nation is seeing the beneficial effects of his products.

A few years ago the two of us formed a team intent on talking to conservation-minded groups around the country. Malcolm talked about his findings on how to create healthy soil. I talked about how we have used his methods, and those of other people who believe in sustainable agriculture, to promote the growth of native grasses and healthier riparian areas on our ranch. We had a very interesting time together, and I learned so much from him along the way. Unfortunately, ALS brought an end to our travels.

The last time Malcolm spent the night with us, we sat outside and gazed in wonder at the Milky Way. Where he lives in San Antonio, the lights of the city have taken the Milky Way from him. He told me as he left that he was coming back so he could see the Milky Way again. I hope he does not wait too long.

September 28, 2006

There is a force within me, more powerful now, that wants to withdraw from everything and let this disease run its course. It is an embarrassment for me to eat in front of other people. When we go anywhere, our trip has to be planned around rest-rooms where Veleda can help me. It is maddening to think that I am rapidly moving toward a state of total dependence on others. This disease not only intends to kill, it wants to humil-iate, cripple, and demoralize before taking its final satisfaction. Yet I know the worst it does is not to me but to those around me. Every day I want to give up, but in the back of my mind I know to do so would be giving in to defeat. I have never done that before.

In the darkness of it all, there are good things that happen. Despite my yearning to be away from everything outside this place, friends break through the barrier. The cards, letters, phone calls, and visits from cherished friends have been blessings to both Veleda and me. This experience has also enabled me and my siblings Larry and Patty to rediscover the love we had for one another as children.

My students in particular have been kind enough to write and remind me of the good things we knew together in an ear-lier time. Friends have come here from great distances. Once they get past the shock of what I look like now, we have mean-ingful conversations and I treasure our moments together. If they have come a great distance, we walk out to the gate together when they are ready to leave. There I notice they all have the same look in their eyes. They know this may be the last time we will see each other, and a struggle to find meaningful words begins. I want to tell them it doesn't matter, what is important is that they came, and I love them for that.

Maybe they will read this piece someday and know how much it meant to me for them to come. "Good friends are like the stars, you can't always see them but you know they're there."[10]

OCTOBER 1, 2006

Today we lay close beside each other in the predawn hours. The warmth from her body took the chill away from the early fall air that had settled around us. She told me about her dream, and we laughed and talked. It was like it always had been, as if nothing had changed.

OCTOBER 17, 2006

Ma Walker is an interesting character I often think about. I'm sure she had another name, but we never knew it, and it would've made no difference anyway. She was Ma to everyone. Though she was in her fifties and I not yet in grade school when we first met, Ma was my first adult friend.

Ma had a small place adjoining our ranch in Lampasas County. She lived alone, she had no man, and didn't need one. She farmed her land with a team of horses, built fences, castrated calves, butchered hogs, and hauled her crops in from the fields with the help of no one, save people like my dad who helped out occasionally.

She was a tall, slender woman with a dignified bearing. As there were no mechanized vehicles on her place, she walked everywhere she went. Sometimes she would walk from her place to ours. I'm not sure how far it was, because you measure distance differently when you're six than you do when you're sixty, but to me it seemed to be a long way. In those days when World War II was coming to an end, with gasoline and tires still rationed, we seldom had any visitors. Whenever I looked down to the end of our lane and saw her making her way toward our house, I was elated. She never came unless she intended to do some serious visiting, which meant she would stay three or four hours and have a meal with us. Sometimes she would stay the night.

Unlike cattlewomen on ranches today, Ma never worked in blue jeans. Despite the rigor of whatever work she might be doing, I never saw her wear anything but a simple cotton dress and a bonnet. Another thing about her attire that set her apart from other people was the fact that whenever she came to visit, she was wearing a cartridge belt and carrying a .22 rifle. If you asked her why she was carrying a gun, she would say something about rattlesnakes, but there was more to it than that. There had been trouble between families in an earlier time, but I was too young to know the particulars. Like everybody else in the area, I sensed she was no person to mess with.

Ma loved to dip Levi Garrett snuff. As with all seasoned snuff dippers, you seldom saw her spit. In fact, unless you knew what you were looking for, you might never know that she was a dipper. Being indoors presented something of a challenge for her. She remedied the problem through the use of a "dippin' stick." This indispensable tool was a hand-fashioned, barbed, live-oak stick that looked something like a short knitting needle. She would dip the stick into her stuff can and then, as though she were a child with a pacifier, keep the stick in her mouth for hours at a time.

Sometimes when we went into town on Saturday afternoon for supplies, she would ride along. If money was not too short, the two of us would go to whatever cowboy movie was playing that day. As I think back, I guess going to the show was one of the few places she went unarmed. I say she was unarmed, but I never knew what she carried in her large purse other than her dippin' paraphernalia, which she put into use as soon as the lights went out.

One of the movies Ma and I saw later inspired a memorable incident that resulted in my getting a paddling. Ma was washing that day, which meant she had a roaring fire going around the cast-iron kettle she used to heat water. On that particular day, I was at her house playing with her nephew Butch. I told him about a strategy the good guys had used in the previous Saturday movie. The good guys had tricked the villains into thinking they were under attack by throwing some cartridges into the campfire.

One thing led to another, and since Ma always had enough cartridges to hold off a Comanche attack, we decided on a reenactment. Butch brought a handful of cartridges from the house, and we threw them into the fire. We then took our positions around the campfire to launch our surprise attack when the fireworks started. We did indeed produce some fireworks. The shell casings started exploding, sending bullet fragments zinging past our positions. This was a real battle. We returned the fire with all our vigor. It was not long before the exploding ordinance attracted Ma's attention. She entered the fray and seizing us boys by our collars, dragged us away from the battleground. The paddling my daddy gave me that night was a major invasion of my comfort zone.

Ma's independence and self-reliance were evident in so many things she did, but the way she used that old black washpot will always stand out in my mind. She obviously used it for washing her clothes, but that was only one of its multiple purposes. She used the pot to make her own lye soap. She usually cut her soap up into large pie-shaped wedges that I thought had an exotic smell. The soap smelled a lot better than it felt when she used it to scrub you down at night.

Beyond washing and soapmaking, the washpot also served Ma as a food processor. As soon as she had gathered her corn each year, she shelled a washpot full of corn and through a series of concoctions I never understood, a few days later she had a winter's supply of hominy.

As in most of the Hill Country, wild mustang grapes grew in abundance on her place. Each summer when the grapevines bore their fruit, the old washpot became Ma's grape press. The grapes were pulverized and the juice strained away. The juice, when poured over chipped ice from the icebox, was a delightful August drink. Hot biscuits, dripping with fresh butter and filled with her homemade grape jelly, would rival anyone's culinary art.

The washpot also played a primary role in processing Ma's winter meat supply. Generally in those days, families helped one another when the time came to butcher hogs each year. Sometimes Ma helped us, and later we would return the favor. The old washpot was first used to heat the scalding water for carcass preparation, as the bristly hair needed to be scraped away. My dad always said Ma was the best hog scraper he ever saw. After all the meat was cut up, the last thing we did was to render the lard in the washpot. The lard (low-cholesterol, I am sure) served as the year's supply of cooking oil, as well as a preservative for the sausages packed away in jars or crocks.

Ma's magic with the washpot was just one set of skills she possessed. Her skills as a gardener, farmer, hunter, and forager are stories in themselves. You don't see many self-reliant people like her anymore. I wouldn't say that she chose the simple life, because she had never known anything different. There is no doubt, however, that in the simplicity of her life, she found joy and meaning. For her there was dignity in all that work, and from what I observed, she found harmony in the world about her. I think maybe that is what set her free—freedom from many of the demons contemporary Americans invite into their lives.

I wish there were more people like her today. Given the independence of the American spirit, I am sure there are individuals like her out there somewhere, but they are hard to find. They stand in stark contrast to the great majority of Americans who have chosen a pompous lifestyle and who are largely dependent on others for essential services and goods.

I have often wondered how, as a nation, we would survive the Armageddon experience history has promised us. I shudder to think how the masses I see in the malls and the supermarkets would respond to a situation demanding their own self-reliance. Could it be that the price we will have paid for becoming the world's most technologically advanced and affluent society is that we are now incapable of sustaining our own lives in times of great peril?

OCTOBER 19, 2006

The more we know, the more we know we don't know.
—Abraham Lincoln[11]

A physician I know spent some of his youth exploring the Mexican Yucatan Peninsula. In this place of the ages, the Aztec and Mayan civilizations flourished before the time of Christ. Today, the remnants of their civilizations continue to provide searchers with insights into some of life's great mysteries.

While he was there, the physician became totally fascinated by a story about a village healer. One day a Yucatan mother had noticed a sore developing on the arm of her young daughter. She took her daughter to one of the local physicians, who told her not to worry because the little girl only had a bacterial infection. She was given some salve to put on the sore and told it would be healed in two weeks.

In two weeks the sore was not healed; in fact, it was worse, so she took her daughter to another physician in a larger town. The new physician diagnosed the problem as a bacterial infection, gave the mother some salve and told her the problem would be cured in two weeks. In two weeks, when the problem had not gone away, the mother became very concerned and traveled to Mexico City seeking treatment for her daughter at a major medical center. There, she was given the same diagnosis and a salve to put on the sore and told her daughter would be cured in two weeks.

The mother returned to her little village, and when two weeks went by with no improvement, she began to panic. It was at that point she decided to take her daughter to a shaman, a village healer, who lived nearby. The shaman examined the sore on the little girl's arm, gave her mother some salve, and told them it would be gone in two weeks. In two weeks the sore disappeared.

An elated young mother then returned to the shaman to thank him for what he had done. While she was there, she told him of her frustration with the others who treated her daughter. The shaman smiled gently, put his hand on her arm and said, "Be patient with them; they have been doing this for only two hundred years whereas we have been doing it for over a thousand years."

At times we associate wisdom with a person's title within an organization, degrees held, and honors conferred. Ultimately I believe wisdom is not so much a state of being, as it is a process of becoming. Yes, there are triumphal moments we should savor when milestones of achievement in our lives are reached, but real wisdom comes not from the learning plateaus we reach, but from our continuing pursuit of the mysteries of peaks and valleys beyond. Lincoln told us long ago that "the more we know, the more we know we don't know." Could it be that the highest form of ignorance exists in learned people, contemptuous of the collective wisdom of the ages and all views different from their own?

OCTOBER 23, 2006

My legs, which carried me around the track so many times in high school and college, now struggle to get from one room to the other. I try not to see this as an act of betrayal, but of all my body parts, my legs have always been the strongest. I would likely never have gone to college had I not been lucky enough to receive a track scholarship. After college and long before the jogging craze started, I continued to run. I well remember the strange looks I received in the early days when I jogged along streets where the only other people you saw running were children. Running for me was always an exhilarating experience that tired my body but liberated my mind from many of the pressures I felt at work.

When we were in Greece, I had the opportunity to go to Olympia, the site where our Olympic Games have their origin. I walked through the tunnel the athletes used to enter the field and there before me was the place that marked history. In that moment I did not see the hundreds of camera-laden tourists wearing sunshades and shorts; instead I chose to see the ancient warriors who had come to this field of competition. The naked athletes raced past me on the field. (None of the participants were permitted to wear clothes for fear of their hiding weapons.) The sweat-soaked wrestlers grappled with each other, looking for the moment to throw their opponents to the ground. I saw the ancient discus spun into the air by men with massive shoulders and arms. On the knoll surrounding the field of competition, thousands of spectators observed the games and cheered for their favorite athletes. It was 526 BC again, and I was there.

I ran onto the track and began my most memorable run among the spirits that linger there. I ran to the end of the straightaway track and, as with the original runners, turned and sprinted back to the starting line. I could hear the roar of the crowd, the footsteps of the other runners about me, and the groans that always come from tiring athletes nearing the finish line.

Veleda and the friends who were with us saw me cross the finish line in the twenty-first century. Some of them wildly cheered my performance; others jeered because I had refused to run in the nude. None of them understood I was running in another time.

OCTOBER 24, 2006

My doctors told me from the start that I was going to die, but for thirty months I have never *felt* like I was going to die. I can't say that any longer. I have nausea much of the time now, and my strength seems to be going at the speed of light. Writing this manuscript with the help of my voice-activated computer program now exhausts me within an hour, and I wonder how much longer my voice will hold out. I now fear I will never be able to complete this work. Even so, I will press on and hope there is enough left in me to finish this last race.

JANUARY 3, 2007

Our family has grown by two feet. Elisabeth Rose Boyd made her debut today at 8:35 a.m. We are so delighted that the life cycle continues and sit in wonder at the miracle of birth. My hope is that she will be a searcher for the great truths in life. My prayer is that she will discover that true happiness lies not in what you receive, but in what you give.

JANUARY 15, 2007

One of the most forbidding places on this planet is a stretch of land in northern Nevada between the Carson and Humboldt Rivers. Known as the Forty-Mile Desert, it was the most dreaded part of the California Trail. The trail across the desert's dry alkaline flats is marked by hundreds of graves and a wide array of discarded items left in the wake of the pioneers who sought to cross the desert here. At one point, water gushes forth from a spring along the trail, but it is boiling-hot geyser water. Many unfortunate travelers, desperate for water, came to this spot only to die from thirst because the water was too hot to drink.

Eventually someone placed a barrel near the spring, and the unwritten code of the trail thereafter was for each traveler to fill the barrel with water so that the next passerby would find

water cool enough to drink. Those who traveled on without fill-
ing the barrel put those who followed them in great peril.

In many respects today, there are people who choose to fill
the barrel for those who follow, but unfortunately there are others
who choose to leave the barrel empty. Most of us never forget the
"barrel fillers" we have known. Their actions are etched into our
minds forever and their legacies often shape history.

Dr. Jack Logan always left the barrel full. I first knew him
as a country dentist who lived in Conway, Arkansas. When he
was not at work in his practice, he gave much of his life to the
local Boy Scout troop and his church. He was the best scout
leader I ever knew. He usually spent one weekend out of the
month with his boys somewhere in the Ozarks. He had a remarkable ability to interest in scouting young men who might easily
have chosen less desirable outlets for their energies. I don't
know how many Eagle Scouts he prepared, but the number was
surely large, and my son Chad was one of them. His approach
to scouting was very unorthodox. Given some of the rumors I
heard, it may be best parents not know all of the adventures the
scouts had on their outings, but they had great fun and they
loved Jack Logan.

In April of last year Jack and some members of his church
went on a mission trip to Nicaragua. In that remote part of the
world his skills as a dentist were incredibly useful, and I suspect
his deep religious faith did much more for the people than just
fix teeth.

When the mission trip was complete, Jack and another mis-
sionary from Conway, Bert Alexander, decided to stay over and
do some fishing. They joined a boatload of locals and set forth
on a fishing trip on Lake Nicaragua. One of the largest lakes in
the hemisphere, Lake Nicaragua is subject to sudden and severe
storms. Sometime after the trip got under way, the craft was
swamped by a storm and those aboard were cast into the lake.
Some of them drowned immediately. Jack, Bert Alexander, and
two young Nicaraguans managed to catch a floating ice chest
from the boat. The four of them stayed afloat for twenty-four
hours by holding on to the chest. In time, however, it became
obvious that a small chest could not support the four individu-

als indefinitely. At that point Jack took off his watch and gave it to one of the Nicaraguans. He then turned to Bert and said something to the effect of "I have lived longer than you, and you need to take care of the boys." He then turned loose of the ice chest and disappeared into the waters of the lake.

As the day wore on, conditions for the three survivors continued to worsen. Seeing that the three of them could not stay afloat, Bert Alexander also chose to give up his grip on the ice chest and he too was swallowed up by the waters. The next day the two young Nicaraguans were rescued.

I wish I had the words to write some kind of epitaph for Jack Logan, but the way he chose to die says more for the man than any feeble words I might be able to muster. I, and I suspect a great number of other people, will remember Dr. Jack Logan and Bert Alexander as barrel fillers.

A few years ago Veleda and I had the opportunity to attend a conference where Dr. Temple Grandin was the keynote speaker.[12] Dr. Grandin is a professor of animal science at Colorado State University and an internationally acclaimed author and authority on the design of equipment for the humane management of livestock. She has published more than three hundred articles in professional journals, and her book *Animals in Transition* made the *New York Times* Best-Sellers list. She is highly sought after as a speaker.

For most people who have read her books, heard her lectures, or seen her on numerous television programs, Dr. Grandin's rise to prominence in her field is remarkable in and of itself. There is another story here, though. Temple Grandin is autistic. When Temple was three years of age, her parents were told she had autism and that she should be institutionalized. Then, and too often now, the disorder was seen as an untreatable condition in patients who were expected to live out meaningless lives with diminished ability to communicate or show affection.

Dr. Grandin became one of the first people in history to talk to the world from the other side of autism. Her remarkable story is detailed in her book *Emergence: Labeled Autistic*. She attributes her emergence from the shackles of autism primarily to early therapeutic intervention, the unrelenting will of her parents, who refused to believe she could not improve, and help from an extraordinary mentor. I suspect also that her intrepid spirit has played no small part in what she has been able to accomplish.

Through her speeches and writing, she has been able to bring to light previously unknown information and insights about the effects noise, touch, and visualizations have on those with autism. While she has made incredible progress in fighting her own disorder, she will tell you that her remarkable journey out of the darkness does not mean she has been cured of autism. She still has to deal with many of the demons autism imposes on its victims, but she has been able to cope with them and, in the process, lead a remarkably productive life. She has never denied her diagnosis, but she has refused to accept the limitations others would define for her. For those families who have autistic children, Dr. Grandin is a barrel filler. The barrel she leaves behind is filled with hope and possibilities for an escape from despair.

My neighbor Ruben Geistweidt is also a barrel filler. Now in his eighty-second year, he and his wife, Doris, have a sizable ranching operation. Ruben has been responsible for managing the family's ranch since the day his father died, when he was twelve years old. Life has denied him some of the freedoms and opportunities others his age enjoyed, but you would never know it by talking with him.

At social gatherings or in the churchyard, when ranchers get together to whittle and talk about the weather or other goings-on, I'm always curious as to what Ruben has to say. Time and time again, whenever I or someone else might paint a bleak future scenario, it would be countered by an optimistic comment from Ruben.

He is not a naive person, for he has seen the toll taken by sudden death, the fury of Texas droughts, and depressed livestock markets. During prolonged droughts, he has known the fiery heat from the propane burners he must use to burn the thorns from the prickly pear so that his cattle can eat the cactus. When times were rough and he could not make ends meet, he knew what it was like to work all day as a carpenter and then spend some of the night and the weekends trying to catch up on his ranch work. From his irregular gait, it is easy to see that every day he lives with the pain of arthritic knees.

It seems to me that Ruben determined long ago that he could be bitter about circumstances or that he could look for the good in whatever he found. It is his quest for the good that makes him so special. If you talk with him for any length of time, one way or another he will communicate to you that he thinks things are going to get better. I laugh with him even when I do not feel like it because he refuses to let gloom settle around him. We seldom ever part company without him saying, "Now you let me know if I can ever help you."

The interesting thing about barrel fillers is that much of the time we never have the chance to pay them back for what they've done. The people on the Forty Mile Desert who found cool water in the barrels filled by others probably never knew their benefactors. The two young men Jack Logan saved by giving his life will never have a chance to thank him. Dr. Temple Grandin will never know a fraction of those with autism she has helped. Fortunately, I have had the opportunity to tell Ruben Geistweidt how much I think of him, but there are so many who will never have a chance to know someone like him. For most of us, we can never repay the barrel fillers because we can't touch the past, but we can touch the future by searching for barrels to fill.

A Final Entry

I have always thought it interesting to note how some people cope with difficult circumstances. In all our lives there will come a time when our inner being will be challenged. That challenge may not come in the dramatic form we read about in the lives of heroes, but it will come.

An extreme example of what I am referring to takes place in the lives of those who seek to become Navy SEALs. Some people believe their rigorous training to be the most difficult ever devised by the military. Many of the trainees make it through the bulk of the demanding program, only to fail the ultimate test called Hell Week.[1]

What is there about a few individuals that enables them to master the obstacles to becoming a Navy SEAL? This question has been the point of numerous research projects conducted by the military and by psychological investigators. It was first assumed that survival would be linked to the incredible physical attributes of trainees. Researchers could find no correlation there. There was no significant physical difference between those who survived and those who failed.

The difference researchers found was in the mind, and in an interesting phenomenon called the Porthole Effect.[2] Those who survived Hell Week learned that pain ultimately resides in the mind and that the mind can control pain. The real you is only a passenger in your body. A person who survives the incredibly difficult demands of Hell Week does so, not because of his physical toughness, but because he "retreats mentally to the inner safety of his body, looking out through his eyes at the hostile world around him as if he were peering through a porthole." Though the mind still functions in the porthole, it chooses to become oblivious to pain. Those who did not find the port-hole almost always dropped out of the program.

A similar finding to that of the Porthole Effect was reported in Viktor Frankl's book *Man's Search for Meaning*.[3] When World War II began, Frankl, a German Jew, along with members of his family were arrested by the Nazi Gestapo. He was eventually separated from his family and spent the next four years in labor camps. In the camps he endured a subhuman environment where torture, beatings, and starvation were part of each day. He began his day in darkness awaiting the order to march through ice and snow to the work site. His greatest fear was that through injury or illness he would be rendered unfit to work and therefore sent to the execution chambers. He slept each night on a plank bed with five other men whose sole source of warmth were human bodies lying side by side under a single blanket.

A large number of people who came to the camp died or were killed by guard brutality. Others, not able to cope with life, "ran to the wire," killing themselves by touching the high-voltage wire at the base of the prison fence.[4] Though no one thrived in these conditions, some people, including Frankl, survived the experience.

Why did they survive? Frankl survived because, from the onset, he found ways to transfer his mind from the hell his body experienced each day. In effect, he also discovered the porthole. He survived because he chose to find some kind of blessing in each day. The blessing might have been the fact that he escaped guard brutality that day, that he could get his swollen feet into his undersized shoes without difficulty in the early morning, or that on the way to the work site he saw something of beauty in nature. He relished those blessings and reflected on them when all of the elements around him were tearing at his body.[5]

In the midst of extreme fatigue and physical pain, Frankl committed to memory the lectures he planned to give when he returned to his position at the university. He thought of the great truths in human history, and eventually came to understand a meaning in life he could have found in no other place. Later he wrote, "The salvation of man is through love and in love....I now understood how a man who has nothing left in the world may still know bliss, be it only for a brief moment, in the contemplation of his beloved."[6]

Ultimately, Frankl survived because he was able to transfer his mind out of this body to a better place. Though he did not know it at the time, his beloved wife was dead, but thoughts of her sustained him when all other forces in his life were trying to bring him down.

In *Companions of the Blest*, I described how I hoped I would die. The description is of the night an old rancher passes away:

> Just before he went to bed that night, he had hobbled out on the porch to gaze onto a landscape bleached by a Comanche Moon. In the bright light he could see the white cliffs of Sentinel Mountain, and in the elm tree toward the rock fence he could clearly see a screech owl silhouetted against the moon. "It's a mighty fine night," the old man said aloud to himself, for at that moment it seemed that he could see beyond the darkness. Later he would hear the Seth Thomas clock his grandfather had given him chime three times. His last breath was from the cool river breeze that blew up from the Llano and through the open windows into his bedroom.[7]

The old man in the book died a rancher's death, free from the indignities of nursing care, in the home he loved, breathing good air through an open window.

I am now beginning to experience the pain that settles over the body in the latter stages of ALS. Eventually I will become a quadriplegic unable to communicate or voluntarily move any part of my body. Strangely enough, though, surrounded by useless parts, my mind will remain alive. My hope is that some system in my body will short-circuit and spare me this imprisonment, but I can't depend on that. I spend more time now than before thinking about this eventuality.

I am uncertain as to how I will be able to cope with the future, but I do have a plan; even if this disease has its way with me, my fate will nonetheless be different. No one who sees me then should be distressed by my expressionless eyes. Remember, "the real you is only a passenger in your body." While my mind may still reside in my body, I will not be home. It will be in another place with work to do.

There were so many lectures I never gave while I was at the university. I will give them now, and I will do so in an unrestrained environment. I always wanted to teach courses outside my discipline, so I will be free to explore philosophy, psychology, and religion. The other novel I wanted to write about the Texas frontier will now take shape. This time I will not be faced with publishers' deadlines.

As if my mind were a camera, I am now collecting mental images of people I care about. Christian, Mariah, Thomas, Elisabeth Rose, and all those I love have been captured for inclusion in an album I will review daily. Through those images we will take journeys together to visit the happy times from the past, and though I can't go with them into the future, I will knock on its door for them.

Finally, I take comfort from Frankl's words that "a man who has nothing left in the world may still know bliss, be it only for a brief moment, in the contemplation of his beloved." I am not sure a person in ordinary circumstances, a person who has never lived under the dark cloud, can fully appreciate this message. I have had the love of a wonderful woman, and no diseased body can take that from me. My contemplation of the depths of the love we shared gives me confidence my memories will sustain me in whatever future circumstance comes.

My life has been enormously blessed.

Postscript

Christian, Mariah, Thomas, Elisabeth Rose, as I said at the start of this work, I hoped to capture, from my own imperfect life, lessons that might be of use to you in the future. My journey since then has taken me down a number of roads I never expected to follow. It may be that along the way, I became not the teacher, but the real student. As I think back on this experience, I know it has given me a much greater appreciation for all things. For that, I am so very grateful, and I suppose I have you to thank.

For me, one of the most memorable things I found in my research for *A Servant Leader's Journey* came the day I stumbled onto the words of our ancestor Roland Taylor. Two days before he was martyred in 1555, he was allowed to briefly speak with his family. His moving message to them transcends all generations. It is a message of parting and I leave it for you, your Oma, and your moms and dads. I hope you will share it with your children.

> I say to my wife, and to my children, The Lord gave you unto me, and the Lord hath taken me from you, and you from me: blessed be the name of the Lord! I believe that they are blessed which die in the Lord. God careth for sparrows, and for the hairs of our heads. I have ever found Him more faithful and favorable, than is any father or husband. Trust ye therefore in Him by the means of our dear Savior Christ's merits: believe, love, fear, and obey Him: pray to Him, for He hath promised to help. Count me not dead, for I shall certainly live, and never die. I go before, and you shall follow after, to our long home. (Roland Taylor, February 7, 1515)[1]

Epilogue

On April 8, 2007, Jim had to be hospitalized for a respiratory infection. During the several days that he was there, we were forced to face some harsh realities. First, the doctors said that he would have to be on his noninvasive, BiPAP breathing machine full time. Also, they said we needed to think about contracting with home health and hospice to help with his care. I had told the doctors earlier that our family would not consider a nursing home facility, so they said that we would have to decide where he would spend whatever time he had left.

The small town house that we had in Fredericksburg for only occasional use had little meaning to Jim. When we asked him where he wanted to spend his remaining time, he quickly chose our ranch home. Although the remoteness of the location caused some concern, I knew that his joy in being there far outweighed the risk of faraway medical help.

The day we brought him home, we both knew that he would never again leave the ranch until his death. The emotionally charged atmosphere was tempered by our happiness at being on our homeplace again.

Thankfully we had a large bedroom that easily accommodated his hospital bed and other necessary equipment, and the grandchildren's art scattered about the room added cheer to the place. Our son Chad put a deer feeder outside one of the large bedroom windows, allowing Jim to view the development of the bucks during the next five months—from the formation of their velvet-coated antlers to the fully developed finished ones. A hummingbird feeder brought many of the small birds daily. When the cattle came to the pens to drink water, he could check on their condition. Our son Jeff videoed many places on the ranch that were special to Jim, and visitors thereafter were treated to the show. Mornings, I would read the Bible, books, or articles to him. Many evenings, the family would gather in our bedroom to view a movie, sports event, or documentary, replete with the requisite popcorn.

Early in September, we knew that the end was imminent. Even the breathing machine could not compensate completely for the loss of muscle tone relating to his respiration, and he refused any invasive breathing device. ALS had made him a quadriplegic, but it never took away his voice as he had feared it would.

On September 22, with his family gathered around him and his faithful dog Belle lying by his bedside, Jim Boyd peacefully left this world. He died surrounded by the people he loved on the land he loved. He couldn't have scripted it better.

—*Veleda Boyd, his wife of forty-six years*
December 2007

Notes

Introduction

1. Henry David Thoreau, "Walden," in *The American Tradition in Literature*, 7th ed., ed. George Perkins et al. (New York: McGraw-Hill, 1990), 626.

2. Ernest Hemingway, *The Old Man and the Sea* (New York: Scribner's, 1980), 59–60.

3. William Shakespeare, *Henry IV, Part II*, act 5, scene 3.

Chapter 1

1. Robert Greenleaf, *The Servant as Leader* (Indianapolis: Robert Greenleaf Center, 1991), 1–37.

2. Nancy Larner Ruschman, "Servant-leadership and the Best Companies to Work for in America," in *Focus on Leadership*, ed. Larry C. Spears and Michele Lawrence (New York: Wiley, 2002), 123–40.

3. Edwin Friedman, *A Failure of Nerve: Leadership in the Age of the Quick Fix* (Bethesda, MD: Edwin Friedman Estate/Trust, 1999), 132.

4. Jim Collins, *Good to Great* (New York: HarperCollins, 2001), 28.

5. Jim Collins, "Level 5 Leadership: A Triumph of Humility and Fierce Resolve," *Harvard Business Review* (January 2004): 21–31.

6. Joshua Wolf Shenk, "The True Lincoln," *Time*, July 4, 2005, 43.

7. Carl Sandburg, *Abraham Lincoln: The Prairie Years and the War Years* (New York: Harcourt Brace Jovanovich, 1954), 589.

8. Collins, "Level 5 Leadership," 21–31.

9. Margaret Truman, *Harry S. Truman* (New York: Morrow, 1973), 972.

10. Robert A. Wilson, ed., *Character above All: Ten Presidents from FDR to George Bush* (New York: Simon & Schuster, 1995), 39–59.

11. Ibid.

12. Portions of this section were previously printed in *Texas School Business*, November–December 2005, 28.

13. Lance Armstrong, *It's Not about the Bike: My Journey Back to Life* (New York: Putnam, 2000), 273.

Chapter 2

1. Nancy Anderson, *Work with Passion: How to Do What You Love for a Living* (Novato, CA: New World Library, 2004), i.

2. Winston S. Churchill, *Blood Sweat and Tears* (New York: Putnam, 1941), 297.

3. Amanda Ripley, Nation, *Time*, November 12, 2005, 35.

4. Edwin Friedman, *A Failure of Nerve: Leadership in the Age of the Quick Fix* (Bethesda, MD: Edwin Friedman Estate/Trust, 1999), 117.

5. Franklin D. Roosevelt, first inaugural address (March 4, 1933) http://www.bartleby.com/124/pres49.html.

6. George Washington, *The Writings of George Washington: Being His Correspondence, Addresses, Messages and Other....* (Boston: American Stationer's, 1837), 235.

7. Joseph M. Siracusa and David Coleman, *Depression to Cold War: A History of America from Herbert Hoover to Ronald Reagan* (Westport, CT: Praeger, 2002), 1–44.

8. Jack Lowe, "Trust: The Invaluable Asset," in *Insights on Leadership*, ed. Larry C. Spears (New York: Wiley, 1998), 68–76.

9. Paul Johnson, *Napoleon* (New York: Penguin Putnam, 2002), 165.

10. Hubert Essame, *Patton: As Military Commander* (London: Batsford, 1974), 252; Carlo D'Este, Patton: A Genius for War (New York: HarperCollins, 1995), 638.

11. Portions of this section were previously printed in *Texas School Business*, May 2006, 23.

12. Jacques Ivanoff, "Sea Gypsies of Myanmar," *National Geographic*, April 2005, 36–55.

13. "The Sea Gypsies," segment appearing on *60 Minutes*, CBS, March 20, 2005.

14. Anne Frank, *The Diary of a Young Girl*, www.quoteworld. com, quote no. 4909.

15. J. F. Verbruggen, *The Art of Warfare in Western Europe during the Middle Ages: From the Eighth Century to 1340* (Woodbridge, UK/Rochester, NY: Boydell & Brewer, 1997), 232.

Chapter 3

1. John C. Maxwell, *Developing the Leader within You* (Nashville: Nelson, 1993), 42.

2. Roberta Gilbert, *Extraordinary Relationships: A New Way of Thinking about Human Interactions* (New York: Wiley, 1992), 3.

3. Jim Collins, *Good to Great* (New York: HarperCollins, 2001), 21.

4. Robert Greenleaf, *The Servant as Leader* (Indianapolis: Robert Greenleaf Center, 1991), 9.

5. Maxwell, *Developing the Leader within You*, 42.

6. Edwin Meese, "Abraham Lincoln: Leader for All Ages"

(remarks, Second Annual Lincoln Day Symposium, Claremont Institute, Washington, D.C., February 12, 1998).

7. Alfred Lansing, *Endurance: Shackleton's Incredible Voyage* (New York: Carroll & Graf, 2001), 86.

8. Maxwell, *Developing the Leader within You*, 38.

9. Jim Collins, "Level 5 Leadership: A Triumph of Humility and Fierce Resolve," *Harvard Business Review* (January 2004): 21–31.

10. Ibid.

11. Stephen R. Covey, *The Eighth Habit: From Effectiveness to Greatness* (New York: Simon & Schuster, 2004), 107.

12. Editorial by Teddy Roosevelt, *Kansas City Star*, May 7, 1918.

13. Larry Reynolds, *The Trust Effect* (London: Nicholas Brealey, 1997), 8.

14. Portions of this section previously appeared in *Texas School Business*, January 2006, 21.

15. William F. Buckley, "Capitalism's Boils," *National Review*, April 20, 2005.

16. "Why are sitting members of Congress almost always reelected?" *This Nation*, American Government and Politics Online, www.thisnation.com/question/016.html (accessed November 2, 2006).

17. The Century Foundation, "Updating the 2006 Election Outlook," www.tcf.org/list.asp?type=NC&pub=1272-32k (accessed April 19, 2006).

18. Walter Prescott Webb, *The Great Plains* (Lincoln: University of Nebraska Press, 1981), 10–44.

19. Larry Zellers, *In Enemy Hands: A Prisoner in North Korea* (Lexington: University of Kentucky Press, 1991), 137.

20. *Bonhoeffer*, produced and directed by Martin Doblmeier (Journey Films, 2006).

21. "Martyr for Christ in Hitler's Germany," www.hyper history.net.

22. "Who Is Dietrich Bonhoeffer?" The International Dietrich Bonhoeffer Society, www.dbonhoeffer.org (accessed November 17, 2006).

23. Henry David Thoreau, Walden Classic Quotes Collection, quote no. 9587, www.quotationspage.com.

24. *Legends of the Fall*, directed by Edward Zwick (TriStar Pictures, 1995).

25. Quote from Mother Teresa found at http://www.world ofquotes.com/Mother-Teresa/1/index.html.

26. Quote from Colleen C. Barrett found at http://www. wisdomquotes.com/cat_work.html.

Chapter 4

1. Jim Collins, *Good to Great* (New York: HarperCollins, 2001), 75.

2. James M. Kouzes and Barry Z. Posner, *The Leadership Challenge* (San Francisco: Jossey-Bass, 2002), 112.

3. Kevin Freiberg and Jackie Freiberg, *Nuts! Southwest Airlines' Crazy Recipe for Business and Personal Success* (Austin, TX: Bard Press, 1996), 82.

4. Letter of Anne Sullivan to Sophia C. Hopkins, March 11, 1887, appearing on the Web site of the American Federation for the Blind, www.afb.org.

5. Kouzes and Posner, *Leadership Challenge*, 113.

6. Freiberg and Freiberg, *Nuts!*, 64.

7. Portions of this section were previously printed in *Texas School Business*, March 2006, 23.

8. Sherron Watkins, "Ken Lay Still Isn't Listening," *Time*, June 5, 2006, 35.

9. Robert Greenleaf, *The Servant as Leader* (Indianapolis: Robert Greenleaf Center, 1991), 7.

10. *Walk the Line*, directed by James Mangold (First Line Cinema, 2005).

11. Scott Zesch, "The Search for Alice Todd," *Journal of the West* 44, no. 2 (Spring 2005): 73–80.

12. Ibid.

13. Ibid.

Chapter 5

1. Quotation from George Bernard Shaw, listed at http://www.quotationspage.com/quote/692.html.

2. *The Searchers*, directed by John Ford (Warner Bros., 1957).

3. Margaret Bierschwale, *A History of Mason County, Texas through 1964* (Mason, TX: Mason County Historical Commission, 1998), 137.

4. Carter McNamara, "Thinking about Organizations as Systems," adapted from *The Field Guide to Consulting and Organizational Development* (Minneapolis: Authenticity Consulting, 2007), available at www.managementhelp.org/org_thry/org_sytm.htm.

5. Malcolm Beck, *Lessons in Nature* (Austin, TX: Acres USA, 1991), 69.

6. L. E. Drinkwater, P. Wagoner, and M. Sarrantonio, "Legume-Based Cropping Systems Have Reduced Carbon and Nitrogen Losses," *Nature* 396, November 19, 1998, 262–65, available at www.nature.com.

7. Quotation from Chief Seattle listed at http://thinkexist.com/quotes/chief_seattle.

8. Kevin Freiberg and Jackie Freiberg, *Nuts! Southwest Airlines' Crazy Recipe for Business and Personal Success* (Austin, TX: Bard Press, 1996), 96.

9. McNamara, "Thinking about Organizations as Systems."

10. The source of this quotation is discussed at http://jcsage pub.com/cgi/content/abstract/45/4/371.

11. Edwin Friedman, *A Failure of Nerve: Leadership in the Age of the Quick Fix* (Bethesda, MD: Edwin Friedman Estate/Trust, 1999), 176.

12. Andrew Weil, *Spontaneous Healing: How to Discover and Embrace Your Body's Natural Ability to Maintain and Heal Itself* (New York: Ballantine, 1995), 226.

13. Per Seyersted, *Kate Chopin: A Critical Biography* (Baton Rouge/London: Louisiana State University Press, 1980), 46.

14. David McCullough, *Truman: Character above All* (New York: Simon & Schuster, 1992), 843.

15. Carlo D'Este, *Patton: A Genius for War* (New York: Harper-Collins, 1996).

16. Daniel Goleman, *Primal Leadership: Realizing the Power of Emotional Intelligence* (Boston: Harvard Business School Press, 2002), 172.

17. "Boston Red Sox: A Tribute to Williams," from the Boston Red Sox Web site, http://boston.redsox.mlb.com/NASApp/mlb/bos/history/bos_history_williams.jsp (accessed December 5, 2006).

18. Ibid.

19. Leigh Montville, *Ted Williams: A Biography of an American Hero* (New York: Doubleday, 2004).

20. Quote obtained from Joe Ely's Web site, www.ely.com.

21. "Weekend Edition," interview with Irma Thomas, National Public Radio, July 1, 2006.

Chapter 6

1. Kahlil Gibran quotation available at http://www.famouspoetsandpoems.com/poets/kahlil_gibran/poems/2372.

2. Roy Bedichek, *Adventures with a Texas Naturalist* (Austin: University of Texas Press, 1947), 63–65.

3. Thomas Gray quotation available at http://www.thomasgray.org/cgi-bin/display.cgi?text=elcc.

4. Julius DeVos, ed., *The Hilda United Methodist Church through 125 Years, 1862–1987* (Mason, TX: Hilda United Methodist Church, 1987), 1–5.

5. Japanese proverb available at http://thinkexist.com/search/searchquotation.asp?search=none+of+us+is+as+smart+as+all+of+us&q.

6. Mark Twain quotation available at http://www.online-literature.com/twain/1314/.

7. John Foxe, *Book of Martyrs* (Kensington, PA: Whitaker House, 1981), 214–35.

8. Dr. C. Matthew McMahon, "Memoirs of Reformers," from the Web site *A Puritan's Mind*, http://apuritansmind.com/Reformation/MemoirsReformers/MemoirsRowlandTaylor

9. Dick Richardson and Pat Richardson, *Soil Biological Primer* (Ankeny, IA: Soil and Water Conservation Society, 2000), 4.

10. Quotation available at http://www.famous-quotes.net/Quote.aspx?Good_friends_like_stars_always_see_them_know_there.

11. Roy Basler, ed., *The Collected Works of Abraham Lincoln*, vol. 2 (Piscataway, NJ: Rutgers University Press, 1953), 323.

12. John Kuhn, "An Interview with Temple Grandin," *Harvard Brain* 7 (Spring 2000) http://www.hcs.harvard.edu/~husn/BRAIN/vol7-spring2000/grandin.htm; Temple Grandin, "My Experience with Visual Thinking Sensory Problems and

Communication Difficulties," June 2000, www.autism.org/temple/visual.html.

A Final Entry

1. Douglas C. Waller, *The Commandos: The Inside Story of America's Secret Soldiers* (New York: Dell, 1986), 114.

2. Ibid, 115.

3. Viktor E. Frankl, *Man's Search for Meaning* (New York: Washington Square Press, 1959), 55.

4. Ibid, 36.

5. Ibid, 67.

6. Ibid, 57.

7. Jim Boyd, *Companions of the Blest* (Austin, TX: Eakin, 2002), 221.

Postscript

1. John Foxe, *The Acts and Monuments of John Foxe: A New and Complete Edition*, vol. 8, ed. Stephen Reed Cattley (London: R. B. Seely and W. Burnside, 1965), 100–101.

Bibliography and Other Sources

Books and Articles

Anderson, Nancy. *Work with Passion: How to Do What You Love for a Living*. Novato, CA: New World Library, 2004.

Armstrong, Lance. *It's Not about the Bike: My Journey Back to Life*. New York: Putnam, 2000.

Basler, Roy, ed. *The Collected Works of Abraham Lincoln*, vol. 2. Piscataway, NJ: Rutgers University Press, 1953.

Beck, Malcolm. *Lessons in Nature*. Austin, TX: Acres USA, 1991.

Bedichek, Roy. *Adventures with a Texas Naturalist*. Austin: University of Texas Press, 1947.

Bierschwale, Margaret. *A History of Mason County, Texas through 1964*. Mason, TX: Mason County Historical Commission, 1998.

Boston Red Sox. "A Tribute to Williams." Available at http://boston.redsox.mlb.com/NASApp/mlb/bos/history/bos_history_williams.jsp (December 5, 2006).

Boyd, Jim. *Companions of the Blest*. Austin, TX: Eakin, 2002.

———. "The Gift of Trust" (part 1). *Texas School Business* (January 2006).

———. "Leaders Worth Following." *Texas School Business* (November–December 2005).

———. "The Power of Presence." *Texas School Business* (May 2006).

Buckley, William F. "Capitalism's Boils." *The National Review*, April 20, 2005.

Churchill, Winston S. *Blood, Sweat and Tears*. New York: Putnam, 1941.

Collins, Jim. *Good to Great*. New York: HarperCollins, 2001.

———. "Level 5 Leadership: A Triumph of Humility and Fierce Resolve." *Harvard Business Review* (January 2004).

Covey, Stephen R. *The Eighth Habit: From Effectiveness to Greatness.* New York: Simon & Schuster, 2004.

D'Este, Carlo. *Patton: A Genius for War.* New York: HarperCollins, 1996.

DeVos, Julius, ed. *The Hilda United Methodist Church through 125 Years, 1862–1987.* Mason, TX: Hilda United Methodist Church, 1987.

Drinkwater, L. E., P. Wagoner, and M. Sarrantonio. "Legume-Based Cropping Systems Have Reduced Carbon and Nitrogen Losses." *Nature* 396, November 19, 1998.

Essame, Hubert. *Patton: As Military Commander.* London: Batsford, 1974.

Foxe, John. *The Acts and Monuments of John Foxe: A New and Complete Edition*, vol. 8. Edited by Stephen Reed Cattley. London: R. B. Seely and W. Burnside, 1965.

———. *Book of Martyrs.* Kensington, PA: Whitaker House, 1981.

Frankl, Viktor E. *Man's Search for Meaning.* New York: Washington Square Press, 1959.

Freiberg, Kevin, and Jackie Freiberg. *Nuts! Southwest Airlines' Crazy Recipe for Business and Personal Success.* Austin, TX: Bard Press, 1996.

Friedman, Edwin. *A Failure of Nerve: Leadership in the Age of the Quick Fix.* Bethesda, MD: Edwin Friedman Estate/Trust, 1999.

Gilbert, Roberta. *Extraordinary Relationships: A New Way of Thinking about Human Interactions.* New York: Wiley, 1992.

Goleman, Daniel. *Primal Leadership: Realizing the Power of Emotional Intelligence.* Boston: Harvard Business School Press, 2002.

Grandin, Temple. "My Experience with Visual Thinking Sensory Problems and Communication Difficulties." www.autism.org/temple/visual.html (June 2000).

Greenleaf, Robert. *The Servant as Leader.* Indianapolis: Robert Greenleaf Center, 1991.

Griswold, Eliza. "Sea Gypsies." *New Yorker*, January 24, 2005.

Hemingway, Ernest. *The Old Man and the Sea.* New York: Scribner's, 1980.

International Dietrich Bonhoeffer Society. "Who is Dietrich Bonhoeffer?" www.dbonhoeffer.org.

Ivanoff, Jacques. "Sea Gypsies of Myanmar." *National Geographic*, April 2005.

Johnson, Paul. *Napoleon*. New York: Penguin Putnam, 2002.

Kouzes, James M., and Barry Z. Posner. *The Leadership Challenge*. San Francisco: Jossey-Bass, 2002.

Kuhn, John. "An Interview with Temple Grandin." *Harvard Brain* 7 (Spring 2000), hcs.harvard.edu/~husn/BRAIN/vol7–spring2000/grandin.htm.

Lansing, Alfred. *Endurance: Shackleton's Incredible Voyage*. New York: Carroll & Graf, 2001.

Lowe, Jack. "Trust: The Invaluable Asset." In *Insights on Leadership*. Edited by Larry C. Spears. New York: Wiley, 1998.

Maxwell, John C. *Developing the Leader within You*. Nashville: Nelson, 1993.

McCullough, David. *Truman: Character above All*. New York: Simon & Schuster, 1992.

McMahon, C. Matthew. "Memoirs of Reformers." From the Web site *A Puritan's Mind*, http://www.apuritansmind.com/Reformation/MemoirsReformers/MemoirsRowlandTaylor.

McNamara, Carter. "Thinking about Organizations as Systems." Adapted from *The Field Guide to Consulting and Organizational Development*. Minneapolis: Authenticity Consulting, 2007. Available at http://www.managementhelp.org/systems/systems.htm#anchor6250.

Montville, Leigh. *Ted Williams: A Biography of an American Hero*. New York: Doubleday, 2004.

Reynolds, Larry. *The Trust Effect*. London: Nicholas Brealey, 1997.

Richardson, Dick, and Pat Richardson. *Soil Biological Primer*. Ankeny, IA: Soil and Water Conservation Society, 2000.

Ripley, Amanda. Nation. *Time*, November 12, 2005.

Roosevelt, Teddy. Editorial. *Kansas City Star*, May 7, 1918.

Ruschman, Nancy Larner. "Servant-leadership and the Best Companies to Work for in America." In *Focus on Leadership*. Edited by Larry C. Spears and Michele Lawrence. New York: Wiley, 2002.

Sandburg, Carl. *Abraham Lincoln: The Prairie Years and the War Years*. New York: Harcourt Brace Jovanovich, 1954.

Seyersted, Per. *Kate Chopin: A Critical Biography*. Baton Rouge/London: Louisiana State University Press, 1980.

Shakespeare, William. *Henry IV, Part II*.

Shenk, Joshua Wolf. "The True Lincoln." *Time*, July 4, 2005.

Siracusa, Joseph M., and David Coleman. *Depression to Cold War: A History of America from Herbert Hoover to Ronald Reagan*. Westport, CT: Praeger, 2002.

ThisNation.com. "Why are sitting members of Congress almost always reelected?" American Government and Politics Online, www.thisnation.com (accessed November 2, 2006).

Thoreau, Henry David. "Walden." In *The American Tradition in Literature*. 7th ed. Edited by George Perkins et al. New York: McGraw-Hill, 1990.

Truman, Margaret. *Harry S. Truman*. New York: Morrow, 1973.

Verbruggen, J. F. *The Art of Warfare in Western Europe During the Middle Ages: From the Eighth Century to 1340*. Woodbridge, UK/Rochester, NY: Boydell & Brewer, 1997.

Waller, Douglas C. *The Commandos: The Inside Story of America's Secret Soldiers*. New York: Dell, 1986.

Washington, George. *The Writings of George Washington: Being His Correspondence, Addresses, Messages and Other....* Boston: American Stationer's, 1837.

Watkins, Sherron. "Ken Lay Still Isn't Listening." *Time*, June 5, 2006.

Webb, Walter Prescott. *The Great Plains*. Lincoln: University of Nebraska Press, 1981.

Weil, Andrew. *Spontaneous Healing: How to Discover and Embrace Your Body's Natural Ability to Maintain and Heal Itself*. New York: Ballantine, 1995.

Wilson, Robert A., ed. *Character above All: Ten Presidents from FDR to George Bush*. New York: Simon & Schuster, 1995.

Zellers, Larry. *In Enemy Hands: A Prisoner in North Korea*. Lexington: University of Kentucky Press, 1991.

Zesch, Scott. "The Search for Alice Todd." *Journal of the West* 44, no. 2 (Spring 2005).

Other Sources

Bonhoeffer? Directed and produced by Martin Doblmeier. Journey Films, 2006.

CBS Broadcasting. *60 Minutes.* "The Sea Gypsies." Segment airing March 20, 2005.

Legends of the Fall. Directed by Edward Zwick. Tri Star Pictures, 1994.

Meese, Edwin. "Abraham Lincoln: Leader for All Ages." Remarks, Second Annual Lincoln Day Symposium. Claremont Institute, Washington, DC, February 12, 1998.

National Public Radio. Interview with Erma Thomas. July 1, 2006.

Roosevelt, Franklin D. First inaugural address. March 4, 1933. Obtained at http://www.bartleby.com/124/pres49.html.

The Searchers. Directed by John Ford. Warner Bros., 1957.

Sullivan, Anne. Letter to Sophia C. Hopkins. March 11, 1887. Obtained from the Web site of the American Federation for the Blind, www.afb.org.

Walk the Line. Directed by James Mangold. First Line Cinema, 2005.

Additional information on topics addressed in this book may be found at the following Web sites:

www.afb.org

www.bartleby.com

www.ely.com

www.famouspoetsandpoems.com

www.famous-quotes.net

www.jcsagepub.com

www.hyperhistory.net

www.managementhelp.org/systems

www.nature.com

www.online-literature.com

www.quotationpage.com

www.quoteworld.com

www.tcf.org

www.thinkexist.com

www.thisnation.com

www.thomasgray.org

www.wisdomquotes.com